THE
REINCARNATION
LIBRARY

THE HISTORY OF A SOUL

A TALE OF MANY INCARNATIONS

Justin Sterns

AEON PUBLISHING COMPANY
White Plains
2000

First Published 1910

ISBN: 1-893766-08-X

Library of Congress Card Catalog Number:
99-76091

The Reincarnation Library™ takes great care in maintaining the authenticity, and therefore the integrity, of the author's original work. To this end, not one word of the original text has been altered. Please be aware that there may be phrases or characterizations in this book that the modern reader might find offensive. Such material is in no way reflective of the attitude of the publisher of this edition.

PRINTED AND BOUND IN THE UNITED STATES OF AMERICA.

CONTENTS

Have caution, O Soul,
lest you soar on the wings of Desire

To that Height you aspired to reach
—and beyond, to the Fire.

OSRU

A Tale of Many Incarnations

INTRODUCTION

It is not at all necessary to believe the doctrines of Karma and Reincarnation, on which it is based, in order to follow this history of the soul OSRU—known to man as Nero in his most conspicuous incarnation—a history wherein through various lives he reaps as he has sown and slowly rises to a height of character where right at last seems greater to him than might. But it is, of course, very essential to understand these beliefs.

Briefly, then, Karma is the doctrine (held by something like three-fourths of the inhabitants of the world) that each one reaps the fruits of his own deeds, good or bad, at the same time learning through his suffering to be unwilling to inflict similar pain on another. The drift being ever upward, each learns by doing what he desires to do—and taking the consequences—to discriminate between good and evil and to desire the good.

Reincarnation, which is always believed in where Karma is accepted, provides the opportunity for reaping the fruits of one's deeds and desires. The main tenet of Reincarnation is known to every one, namely: That we live repeatedly, taking up the business of growing better each time at that point where we left off.

In brief, Karma is the Christian doctrine, "Whatsoever a man soweth, that shall he also reap." And Reincarnation is merely the means to that end.

There is only one more point which may not be generally understood. The reincarnating ego is sexless; taking form in whatever environment, and with whichever sex provides the best opportunity for its next lesson.

FOREWORD

I leaned from the low-hung crescent moon and grasping the west-pointing horn of it looked down. Against the other horn reclined, motionless, a Shining One and looked at me, but I was unafraid. Below me the hills and valleys were thick with humans, and the moon swung low that I might see what they did.

"Who are they?" I asked of the Shining One. For I was unafraid.

And the Shining One made answer:

"They are the Sons of God and the Daughters of God."

I looked again, and saw that they beat and trampled each other. Sometimes they seemed not to know that the fellow-creature they pushed from their path fell under their feet. But sometimes they looked as he fell and kicked him brutally.

And I said to the Shining One:

"Are they *all* the Sons and Daughters of God?"

And the Shining One said: "All."

As I leaned and watched them, it grew clear to me that each was frantically seeking something, and that it was because they sought what they sought with such singleness of purpose that they were so inhuman to all who hindered them. And I said to the Shining One:

"What do they seek?"

And the Shining One made answer: "Happiness."

"Are they all seeking Happiness?"

"All."

"Have any of them found it?"

"None of those have found it."

"Do they ever think they have found it?"

"Sometimes they think they have found it."

My eyes filled, for at that moment I caught a glimpse of a woman with a babe at her breast, and I saw the babe torn from her and the woman cast into a deep pit by a man with his eyes fixed on a shining yellow lump that he believed to be (or perchance to contain, I know not) Happiness.

And I turned to the Shining One, my eyes blinded.

"Will they ever find it?"

And he said: "They will find it."

"All of them?"

"All of them."

"Those who are trampled?"

"Those who are trampled."

"And those who trample?"

"And those who trample."

I looked again, a long time, at what they were doing on the hills and in the valleys, and again my eyes went blind with tears, and I sobbed out to the Shining One:

"Is it God's will, or the work of the Devil, that men seek Happiness?"

"It is God's will."

"And it looks so like the work of the Devil!"

The Shining One smiled inscrutably.

"It does look like the work of the Devil."

When I had looked a little longer, I cried out, protesting:

"Why has He put them down there, to seek Happiness and to cause each other such unmeasurable misery?"

Again the Shining One smiled inscrutably.

"They are learning."

"What are they learning?"

"They are learning Life. And they are learning Love."

I said nothing. One man in the herd below held me breathless, fascinated. He walked proudly, and others ran and laid the bound, struggling bodies of living men before him, that he might tread upon them and never touch foot to earth. But suddenly a whirlwind seized him and tore his purple from him and set him down, naked among strangers. And they fell upon him and maltreated him sorely.

I clapped my hands.

"Good! Good!" I cried, exultantly. "He got what he deserved!"

Then I looked up suddenly, and saw again the inscrutable smile of the Shining One.

And the Shining One spake:

"They all get what they deserve."

"And no worse?"

"And no worse."

"And no better?"

"How can there be any better? They each deserve whatever shall teach them the true way to Happiness."

I was silenced.

And still the people went on seeking, and trampling each other in their eagerness to find. And I perceived, what I had not fully grasped before, that the Whirlwind caught them up from time to time and set them down elsewhere to continue the Search.

And I said to the Shining One:

"Does the Whirlwind always set them down again on these hills or in these valleys?"

And the Shining One made answer:

"Not always on these hills or in these valleys."

"Where then?"

"Look above you."

And I looked up. Above me stretched the Milky Way and gleamed the stars.

And I breathed "Oh" and fell silent, awed by what it was given to me to comprehend.

Below me, they still trampled each other.

And I asked the Shining One:

"But no matter where the Whirlwind sets them down, they go on seeking Happiness?"

"They go on seeking Happiness."

"And the Whirlwind makes no mistakes?"

"It makes no mistakes."

"It puts them, sooner or later, where they will get what they deserve?"

"Sooner or later, where they will get what they deserve."

Then the load crushing my heart lightened, and I found I could look at the brutal cruelties that went on below me with pity for the cruel.

And the longer I looked the stronger the pity grew.

And I said to the Shining One:

"They act like men goaded."

"They are goaded."

"What goads them?"

"The name of the goad is Desire."

Then, when I had looked a little longer, I cried out passionately:

"Desire is an evil thing!"

But the face of the Shining One grew stern and his voice rang out, dismaying me:

"Desire is not an evil thing."

I trembled, and Thought withdrew herself into the innermost chamber of my heart. Till at last I said:

"It is Desire that nerves men on to learn the lessons God has set?"

"It is Desire that nerves them."

"The Lessons of Life and Love?"

"Of Life and Love."

Then I looked again into the valley, and the load was gone from my heart. And I could no longer see that they were cruel. I could only see that they were learning.

I watched them, one by one, but the Whirlwind always carried them out of sight.

Then I turned to the Shining One beseechingly:

"If I could only follow one when the Whirlwind takes him, and follow him and follow him——"

I looked into the unfathomable, smiling eyes of the Shining One, and my eyes plead with him.

And the Shining One said:

"You shall follow and follow. Choose."

And my eyes fell again upon the earth. There lay the banks of the Nile. I saw a man with the terror of death in his face who ran like the wind of the desert.

And I said to the Shining One:

"I choose him."

And the Shining One said: "So be it," and was gone.

And I found myself on the earth beside that man, and I saw all things whatsoever he did, and the things that befell him, and whenever the Whirlwind took him, it took me also.

Lo! Desire is potent.
But linger; the Path that you choose

Leads, perchance, where the Sun hides his face,
and the Hell-waters ooze.

SHERAU
THE PARASCHITES

Being
Incarnation the First
of the Soul
Osru

Sherau, the paraschites, having made the eight incisions required by law in the body of the most noble Rameses I. fled for his life from the shower of well-directed stones that were his immediate portion.

For his life in very truth, since this was one of those happily rare occasions when the body desecrated by the abhorred knife of the embalmer's most vile but necessary assistant, the paraschites, was that of a Pharaoh. The stones hurled at him were twice the size used by the onlookers to express their rage at the mutilation of the dead body of a slave, or even a citizen. Moreover, the throng in the City of the Dead, that lay across the sacred Nile on the hither bank from Thebes, was many times greater today than on days of less notable embalmings. In fact, if no chance-directed stone of the many that rained about him found its mark and made him even as the great Rameses now was, then indeed had the sheltering arm of the god of the outcast paraschites been over him during his mad race.

Sherau stumbled on into the shelter of the nearest thicket, cursing the fate that had caused him to be born a paraschites, bruised and stinging from the stones that had found him but freer than on some former occasions from downright hurt. He threw himself face downward among the papyrus reeds and laid his forehead on his crossed arms, breathed and shaken by his wild run and trembling with relief. For Fear of Death and Lust of Life had stalked at the right shoulder and at the left of Sherau the paraschites since the hour he knew that the king was dead, and that the doubtful honor of assisting to prepare the royal mummy was to be his.

"Now by the great God Seth," gasped Sherau, under his breath lest any pious Egyptian should hear him call on the name of the god of all evil, "if I had but the power of Rameses, son of Rameses, over the thrower of every stone flung at me this day for just one little hour; one little, little hour! Ah-e! but I would wring their necks! With my two hands I would wring them." And his two hands could have made short work of the necks of most men.

"If I were but Rameses the Living! Ah-e! Ah-e! Ah-e! They should make me sport for a thousand years, those throwers of stones and shouters of evil names. Ah-e!" Sherau was reviving.

He drew himself up furtively, into the most reverential attitude of the praying Egyptian, and sucked in a long breath.

"O Mighty Seth! Give me the power of Rameses—the power of Rameses—the power of Rameses!"

The veins stood out swollen and blue on his neck and forehead, and on his clenched hands, and he prayed without ceasing till he fell over on his side, exhausted.

He roused up when the tumult of the people who followed the chariot of Rameses II. as he returned across the river to Thebes, reached him.

Sherau crept to the edge of the thicket, and lay concealed where the whole sweep of the road for half a mile spread out below him.

His eyes were set wide open, and blazed like the unwinking, jewel eyes of an idol. As he sprawled full length among the reeds he dug his naked toes into the soft, black earth and his hands reached out and clutched all they could hold of the slender papyri and crushed them together savagely. While he watched the passing pageant his lips writhed over his strong, white teeth, making of his face a most wonderful series of gargoyle masks. At any moment, as he beheld the approach and departure of the Pharaoh and his attendants, his head was a fitting model for a heathen idol of the sort they appease with the sacrifice of little children.

Presently Sherau betook himself to his hovel, in the mean quarter where the Thebans allowed such outcasts as paraschites to live, and there ate, drank and made merry with others of his calling because, having mutilated the body of a Pharaoh that day, he was neither a corpse nor a cripple at nightfall, an escape unparalleled since men first became mummies.

But in the middle of the hot and windless night that followed, sleepless in spite of the wine, Sherau left his hut and sought a place he knew on the Nile bank a little beyond the City of the Dead.

Directly he reached the spot he set about what he had come to do, for it was not the aimless restlessness of insomnia that had sent him night-wandering, and it was not the first time, nor the second, nor the tenth, that he had spent the hours before dawn in his present occupation.

He stalked the bushes skillfully until he succeeded in laying hands of violence on a small she-bird with her three young ones. Long practice had made him deft at this. To-night, the male bird escaped. Had the best of luck been his he would have had that also.

Sherau drew from the bushes a small wicker cage in which he put his captives. The young birds presently gave over squawking and the mother bird, worried and wakeful over her changed surroundings, settled again on her nest to make the best of it.

Sherau's eyes sought the moon. It was still an hour too high for safety in his main enterprise. But fair sport could be had in the interval. He threw himself down and tore up the thick vegetation leaving a level, cleared space under his eyes, as he supported himself on his elbow. A luckless dragon fly lit in the little arena. Immediately, Sherau's great hand covered it. Through his fingers he watched its agitated fluttering.

"I am a mightier than Rameses," he muttered. "I am Sherau the Great, king of land and sea. King of the whole world. Every nation is mine or pays me tribute. A thousand slaves in my palace sweat daily in my service. An hundred thousand are building my tomb, that shall be the wonder of the ages. My name shall never be forgotten. I am Sherau the King.

"This slave here," he mumbled on, "hath crossed my path in somewhat. I have cast him in chains. How shall I serve him, that he may feel the displeasure of the King of the World and all my subjects tremble at his fate? Hold! 'Tis a woman slave. See! she flaunts in gauze. I have but wearied of her. Therefore I will graciously spare her life. I will merely strip her of these costly garments of gold embroidered gauze and cast her out—to be the dancing girl of the paraschites. Ah-e! from the palace of Sherau the Great to the dens of the paraschites! That were worse than death!" He caught the dragon fly carefully and held it down firmly by its outspread wings, reveling in its struggles.

"So! my fair one! Thou dost not wish to be shorn of thy finery and leave the palace of Sherau the Emperor? 'Tis thine own fault. With thy great beauty thou shouldst so have charmed me that I would never have parted with thee. Nay, thou mightest have sat on an Empress's throne. 'Tis without use that thou strugglest. By thy mighty master's commands thou art stripped of thy gauds—one by one!"

With the deliberation of an executioner Sherau robbed the creature of its delicate wings and let it go.

"There! Get thee hence and queen it over the paraschites. Ah-e! 'Tis almost too much favor to those dogs that they should have thee! Mayhap some day when other pleasures pall, I will seek thee out in thy den and thou shalt thank thy king that he spared thy life to-night."

He lolled back on his elbow and waited, for Sherau played the game scrupulously by the rules he had made for it. Only those creatures that ventured into the little arena represented the unfortunate objects of the mighty Sherau's displeasure.

Suddenly he leaned forward with stopped breath. A sacred beetle! lo! a sacred beetle! Never before had the power that ruled provided a scarab to become the object of the royal anger.

Sherau the paraschites threw himself flat on his chest in an ecstasy, and reaching forward with both hands caged the new prisoner where it stood. There was not a spark of awe for the holy things of Egypt in him. Instead a tremulous delight and a huge sense of power at being able to torture and finally to slay that which it meant death to an Egyptian to kill, even by accident, if the fact became known.

"An high priest!" whispered Sherau, with sparkling eyes. "An high priest! Now, indeed, hath Sherau the King fit sport!"

Carefully prisoning the beetle with one

hand, with the other he stripped from a reed a fibre of the strength and flexibility of thread. He looped it about his quarry, between the first and second segments, and holding an end in either hand he settled down to gloat over its struggles and to weave great dreams of absolute power out of them, that should trick him into forgetting that he was a dog of a paraschites.

" 'Tis Ami," he muttered, "who bade me prepare the body of that dead dog of a Rameses today. Now shall he get his deserts!"

With dilating nostrils he tormented the insect a while, letting it seem to escape and dragging it rudely back.

"So! Didst thou think to flee the vengeance of thy king, unhappy priest? Nay, now, the hour of thy death is set and written. I do but play with thee a little space, ere I deliver thee over to the executioner. Fit sport for kings! Fit sport for kings!" he muttered.

"Now, now, thou wretched one," impatiently, "if thou wilt not be quiet—we must see what can be done to quiet thee. My hands weary of keeping such constant hold on thy rope."

One by one, he removed the legs of the insect, thrilling at each desecration of the sacred creature as though it were in fact the living body of his enemy, the high priest, that he mutilated.

"Now, at last, thou art content to be quiet, art thou? But thy submission cometh too late to avail thee aught. Thou shouldst have bent the knee to Sherau, and ceased to cross his mighty will, ere, by his orders, thou wert shorn of thy sacred office. His word is given. Thou must die."

He put the beetle through the bars of the wicker cage, and roughly prodded the bird awake. But she refused to touch it. Perhaps the impulse to eat lay dormant in her during the hours belonging to sleep.

"Then will I be thy executioner," snarled Sherau. With a quick jerk he tightened the loop of reed fibre, and directly the body of the sacred scarabæus of the Nile lay dismembered before him.

"Carrion," he muttered, poking it out of sight among the reeds.

He looked at the moon.

"One more! There is time for one more!" he whispered, gluttonously, and settled himself to watch.

"The next shall be Setos, the wine-seller," he mused. "He hath done me an ill turn this day concerning the price of that fourth bottle of wine. 'Twas half water—ah-e! Setos! welcome!" Sherau's long arm shot out in greeting. He grasped by the gorgeous wings the moth that had come unwittingly to play the sorry rôle of Setos.

"Thou goest finely clad, O Setos, charger of

three prices for thy diluted wine! 'Tis simple justice that I should take from thee this gaudy cloak thou gottest by such thievery. There! Henceforth go afoot, and clad in rags. 'Tis properer so. And harken, Setos! Hadst thou not spat upon me for an 'outcast dog of a paraschites' when I told thee of the water in thy wine, then would I have spared thee this further punishment. Seest thou this house of twigs I build thee with mine own hands? Therein shalt thou stay till thou diest of hunger and thirst. For thy sins, O Setos. Ah-e! Setos! Sherau the Mighty is long of arm and strong of hand. Thou wilt never sell poor wine again."

He looked for the third time at the moon, and getting up stretched lustily. His night of pleasure was not half over. If that which was to follow did but equal what was just completed, then would the days of terror he had endured since the death of Rameses be altogether wiped out. He took up the cage of nesting birds and plunged deeper into the thicket.

Presently he reached a small pit covered with a lattice of twigs, and cunningly contrived to escape notice. Many an anxious hour had Sherau spent on the construction of this dungeon, knowing perfectly that discovery would cost him his life. Now, after a thorough reconnoitre, he put in his hand and drew forth his royal prisoner—a starveling kitten some six months old. Of a truth, this Egyptian holdeth nought holy! In his mad lust for power he layeth violent hands on all that is most sacred to his race. Nothing could save an Egyptian who was known to have killed a cat. It is a tremulous joy to Sherau, when life is hardest and he is made most keenly to feel a miserable outcast, to remember that thrice already he has done what not one of his persecuters would dare do—and yet he lives!

There was water at all times in the den of the half-starved kitten, which Sherau had risked his life five months before to steal. Food he brought as he had brought it now, not too often, lest his coming be observed. Moreover, there was vivider delight to be had from the antics of his prisoner when its hunger was keen. Sherau laughed aloud now, as the kitten glared at the birds and began to lash its tail.

He threw himself down again on his belly, with his puppets within sweep of his long arms. And first, disregarding the agony of the awakened mother bird, he took the cat in his brutal hands and looked it over sharply. The creature bore the scars on its thin body of previous torture. Not hunger only did Sherau the Great mete out to his royal prisoner.

"Ah-e! Rameses the Little! Thy namesake is dead. This day have I thrust my knife into him. Shall I therefore do likewise unto thee?—or save thee a while that thou mayest make sport for me? Art hungered, little king? emperor that was? dethroned one? So! then thou shalt kill but not eat! kill but not eat! kill but not eat! Thou that wert king, thou shalt be executioner, despised of the people and profiting not by the deaths of thy victims."

He put the cat back in its hole and turned his attention to the birds.

"Thou first!" to the mother bird, "that thy squawking may cease."

He looped a cord about her neck and under her wings and then, with evil ingenuity, wound another one around her bill so that her fear was no longer audible. Returning her to the cage he bound her offspring in the same way.

"The anger of the mighty Sherau is great," he muttered to them. "Ye slept, and danger threatened the life of the king your master, whom ye were appointed to guard. Treason! Quick death were a thousand times too merciful. Sherau will show the world a king's displeasure. Ye shall die a death not known to man until this day. Ye shall be thrown to the lions. Ah-e! Never again will a soldier of Sherau the King fall asleep at his post."

He took out the starveling cat, and slipping the loop at the loose end of the rope tied round its neck over his wrist, he watched his frantic assaults on the cage, chuckling at the madnesses of terror and hunger being enacted for his pleasure. At length he drew back the cat, and taking out one of the birds held it by its tether, cleverly playing one against the other until, satiated, he permitted the kill.

He threw the bird into the hole and beat the cat off cruelly when he tried to follow, at length taking another bird from the cage and thrusting it almost against his muzzle to distract his attention. So the game went on. But at the third kill, as Sherau beat him off when he tried to follow and eat, the half-crazed kitten turned on him and did quick havoc with his claws. Sherau caught him round the neck, cursing savagely, and almost strangled him. Presently he muttered, loosening his clutch:

"Thou shalt die to-night for this that thou hast done." The blood was streaming from his right hand. "But first complete thy work. There is yet one other needs thy claws. Then will I strangle thee, O Rameses, with this same hand that thou hast torn—as I would I could strangle thy namesake, who sleeps tonight in the bed of his father."

The moon was close on an hour lower when they broke in upon him, the lifeless kitten still hanging limp in his bloodstained hand.

Sherau sprang to his feet at their storm of hostile cries, swinging the kitten defiantly about his head with a loud scream of laughter. Death had come to him, death so certain that the idea of seeking to escape it did not enter his mind. Instead, Fear of Death and Lust of Life stood again at his right shoulder and at his left, and they rent his brain between them so that he went altogether mad.

"I go to the Halls of Osiris," he shouted. "Yea, I go! but come thou with me! I go not alone! not alone! I am Sherau the Mighty, king of the earth and of men. If I go this night to the Halls of the Dead, I go fitly attended. Come with me, thou! and thou! and thou!" He felled them like oxen.

The moon dropped lower and hid behind the thicket, leaving the Nile in starry darkness and Sherau, with four others, lying stark beside the stark kitten.

Lo! Desire is potent.
Behold! What you crave shall be yours,

To your uttermost dream and beyond it.
But Justice endures.

NERO
THE EMPEROR

Being
Incarnation the Second
of the Soul
Osru

The Imperial One awoke refreshed. He had slept like an infant from sunrise to sunrise and now, stretching deliciously like a child and with a child's keen satisfaction in the mere feel of the morning air, he returned to consciousness.

"Of a truth I am indeed as the gods," he murmured languorously, "since not even such a magnificent orgy as that"—his mind swept rapidly over the ten hours that immediately preceded his just-finished slumber—"requires of me the price of aching body and splitting head that mortals commonly pay for their intenser pleasures."

It *was* god-like. He yawned lazily, lost in admiration of himself.

'Twas indeed marvellous that a man could so drain the cup, leave but the dregs, and set it down with a steady hand. Would the day ever come when this iron body of his would fail him—Nay! He was the special care of the Olympians; more, a god himself! 'Twas their ichor in his veins made him thus strong. And his mind, dismissing the subject carelessly dwelt happily, instead, on his last waking hours, reliving them with zest.

At length he raised himself on his elbow and

looked around. The slave who alone remained in his chamber while he slept, crouched cross-legged in his corner, dozing.

Seeing that he slept, Nero chuckled like a mischievous boy about to tickle an unconscious comrade with a straw. Slipping from his bed, his delicious languor dispelled for a moment, he looked about for a fitting instrument of torture.

"By Mercury! the very thing!"

He tore down certain long cords that adorned the costly hangings of his couch, and making a slip-noose he dropped it stealthily over the head of the sleeping man. With the other end in his hand he returned to his bed and stretched himself out luxuriously.

"Now would a few choice spirits were with me to see me give this fellow the lesson he needs," quoth Nero to himself, right merrily. "But no matter. The jest will bear telling." Perhaps it occurred to him, casually, that being alone had its compensations, since it left him a free hand if he chose to embellish the jest in the telling.

He forbore to follow up the joke immediately. It prolonged the pleasure to be got from it, to speculate idly on what the knave would do when he woke him. He cursed softly to himself that there was not so much as one boon companion beside him with whom he could lay a wager about it, nor any way to summon one without waking the sleeping slave.

Presently he tightened the cord cautiously. The man woke and sprang up, clutching at his throat and gasping, mad with terror but not in the least understanding his predicament. Nero threw himself back, shaken by violent spasms of laughter. The creature's antics were excruciating before he saw how things were with him, and if that were possible, twice as funny after. Nero's sides ached.

After a time he made an end of laughing, and the tigerish love of power in him woke up. As a jest the thing was stale, but there was still much sport—much sport.

The laughter died out of his eyes, and a glitter like that in the lidless eyes of a snake about to strike replaced it.

He dragged the slave toward him.

"On thy knees, O Gyges," he thundered, and Gyges, clutching with both hands at the rope that threatened his wind-pipe, dropped to his knees and struggled toward him.

"Nay, on thy belly, by Jupiter!" stormed Nero, and with a sudden jerk he sent him sprawling on his face. "I'll teach thee to sleep at thy post! Not another word, on thy life, till I bid thee speak," as the man attempted to gasp excuses. Half dragged, half crawling, he got near enough to clasp the Caesar's naked feet and cover them with beseeching kisses.

Nero stayed his hand. The black fire in his eyes burned low. The situation was developing beyond its early promise. The Imperial One was smitten, suddenly, with a most brilliant fancy.

"Perchance," he said, carelessly, watching his man through slitted eyes, "perchance I may yet spare thy worthless life. Me-seems thou dost realize the greatness of thy sin. I do bethink me of a fitting deed whereby thou mayest blot it out. Dost desire thy life?"

The man made an inarticulate moan, and redoubled his efforts to bathe the imperial feet with his tears and dry them with his kisses.

"Thou shalt worship me as I were Jupiter himself," proclaimed the august Emperor, unctuously, enraptured with his plan as the details of it developed. "Thou shalt worship with whatsoever ardor thou wilt, desiring of me the gift of thy life. And belike, if thou dost worship with enough true fervor to merit such a boon, mayhap, I say, if thou dost please the god that abideth in me with thy worship,—it may be I shall grant thy trifling request."

The trembling Gyges prostrated himself, and never was Jupiter Ammon *in propria persona* more fervently worshipped. Whenever his ardor slacked for a moment Nero turned away his head with a gesture of impatience, and the quivering wretch, prone on the tessellated marble, quivered yet more, redoubling his efforts to move this stony and indifferent god to pity. Once Nero prompted, "Dost know that prayer, 'O Jupiter, Invincible'?" and Gyges stammered through it, and then through every prayer he could remember that in any wise fitted his case, whoever the god or goddess, changing the name to Jupiter, glibly.

At length, satiated, his Master said, indifferently: "Enough! I give thee thy life," and the spent Gyges fell motionless on his face. But an anger-sharpened: "Hast no thanks to offer?" recalled him to his task, and Nero tasted yet another keen and glorious sensation. Truly, the day began richly! To be a god, and to receive the prayers and thanks of man, was indeed divine.

"Have done!" he murmured at last, with feigned languor. "Thy frenzy irks me. Methinks I begin to understand how the gods are sometimes too worn out by the never ending protestations of the people to grant their prayers. Now bathe me, Gyges, and use that new Persian perfume of roses."

Gyges, with his eyes on Nero's face, essayed tentatively to remove the cord from his neck.

"That thou didst not pray for," said Nero, with childish petulance. "Nay, 'tis too late. I am wearied with thy prayers. Thou shalt go about to bathe and clothe me even as thou art. I have spared thy life. Be content." He gave the cord a playful pull and Gyges a meaning glance. "Today, at least, I shall be well served. If thou dost thy duties carelessly, O Gyges!" He laughed loudly. "By Momus! thy face would make a skeleton shake with mirth. Why doth this visible cord so fret thee, fool? Thou knowest"—the words slid juicily between his teeth, and it seemed as though he must have rolled them as a savory tidbit against his palate—"the life of every man in Rome is in my hands equally with thine. A noose, invisible but strong, lieth about the neck of every one of them, and the end of it lieth here—lieth here"—he opened and closed his hand, suggestively, in the very face of Gyges. "As easily as I could tighten this rope thou wearest necklace fashion—shall I show thee how easily?—just so easily I could have the life of any slave or senator in Rome. An I would I could choose at random—say the hundredth man who spoke to me from this hour—and by Jupiter whom I represent on earth, ere the sun set twice, I could find the pretext to slay. Yea! though he were the greatest in the Empire after me. Now by all the gods! I will yet do that very thing! 'Twere a timely jest wherewith to entertain some favored legate."

Gyges, almost forgetting to tremble now that the imperial attention was diverted from him, laved his body with the costly perfume.

"Ah-h!" breathed Nero ecstatically, inhaling the delicious odor with closed eyes, "see thou command to be bought a goodly store of this fragrance of the Olympians. I, also, am one of them."

He opened his eyes sharply, as he realized that for a full minute he had forgotten his godship, and shot a scrutinizing glance at Gyges, to see if he had dared to forget it also. He scowled as he noted that Gyges had ceased to tremble.

Thereafter, the Imperial One fell silent for the space of time it took to bathe his right arm. Then he began smoothly:

"How long hast thou served me, Gyges?"

The man looked up.

"Since eighty days, Imperial One," he answered, after a rapid calculation.

"Ah!" The Imperial One narrowed his eyes to twain wicked slits. As Gyges met their glance his trembling returned to an extent that wholly satisfied the great Caesar. But at the same time it whetted his appetite.

"Thy predecessor pleased me—but for some forty-three. I sent him to the galleys." Which was true as to the galleys, but a lie as to the time.

"And the slave who bathed me before him—let me think—I believe 'twas but a paltry twenty I endured him. One morning he spilled perfume in my eyes. 'Twas a double sin, for the stuff was costly. He still lies in prison. I had not remembered the vermin again but for thee. Let him rot! But he was a clumsy beast, while thy hands, O Gyges, are like down! Of a truth, thou art a wonder, Gyges! Eighty days! Some god protects thee, Gyges!"

The evil little eyes of the august Emperor opened wide in mocking surprise. They feasted on the shaken wretch who was trying to steady the hands that were like down lest they lose their cunning.

Really sated at last by the sight of the miserable creature's deadly fear, the mood of the Emperor changed.

"The gods give joy when they will," he reasoned. "Not often to such as he, but yet they give it. I will cause him to rejoice also. Then shall I have played the god to the full this day." And pleased with this new conceit of his fertile brain, he promptly carried it out.

"Thou pleasest me well, O Gyges!" he said aloud, in a voice of honey. "I would not take a king's ransom for thee!"

The startled slave, mindful of what had pleased before, broke out into fulsome adulation addressing him as Jupiter till Nero simulating ennui stopped him.

"Enough! Thou delightest to serve me? Thou shalt serve me better than by declaiming idle words, or even than by rubbing perfumes on my chest with thy hands of down. Dost remember that Christian maiden thou didst get for me some time agone? By that god of all thieving, Mercury, I never did suitably reward thy theft of her! What sayest thou? So? Her father hath not ceased to strive to put on thee the blame of it? Let him have care! Nero hath torture chambers for such as babble against his pleasures! But as for thee, thou shalt procure me just such another delectable maiden. Just so lovely and just so unwilling. By Cupid! I tell thee I grieved for three days thereafter, that I had given her that same night to the guard! 'Twas such a blunder as Nero never made before nor will again, I promise thee. But thou shalt find me another, and if she doth make me forget the first one, why, as certainly as Venus hears me say the word I will set thee free. Stay now, I have a merry thought, O Gyges! Thou shalt shut her in the locked garden, that she may think to flee me when I come!" The imperial laugh rang out, pealing through the chamber. "Yea! thou wilt deserve thy freedom, an thou procurest me another such morsel. See thou do it."

The Mighty One's toilet proceeded in silence.

"Methinks," he mused aloud, as Gyges bound the fillet on his hair, "methinks the populace shouted less joyfully than their duty was, when I deigned to show myself to them in procession robed as Jupiter, two days since, or is it three? Insects!" he raged, remembering the occasional insulting silences that had fallen on the throngs. "I would see my chariot wheels pass over any of them, as willingly as I would bid thee smite a buzzing fly. Let them wait! Let them wait! I will yet devise some way to teach them proper reverence for their Emperor! It shall yet be felt by every man in Rome, I am his Master!

"Haste thee, Gyges. I am anhungered."

Lo! Desire is potent.
A Flood swiftly bearing you Thither.

But, passing your Goal without pause,
it will carry you—Whither?

DRAVID
OF THE GALLEYS

Being
Incarnation the Third
of the Soul
Osru

"Come hither, Caius! See this fellow here. By Bacchus, 'tis a pity he is not with the gladiators! Why doth thy Festus waste him on a galley? By all the gods, 'twould make my blood tingle to see him meet that black lion of Abyssinia that slew six at the last games! With a spike, say, or the short broadsword. He is from Gaul, is it not so? I have seen his like in Rome. But never—never—his equal. 'Tis thy trireme, this? Then have him out and let us look at him. What! chained at the waist?"

"Yea, and for good reason! Thou sayest well, he is a marvel. But 'tis plain, O Marcus, thou hast not full measure of thy father's warrior blood, or thou wouldst not make lion-meat of such as he! He is the glory of my trireme. Because of him and the stroke he sets, there is neither trireme nor bireme in all the fleets of Rome can make shift to pass us. His muscles are ductile adamant, lightning for speed and one with the everlasting hills for endurance. And yet he is an old man. Look at his hair, my Marcus. Fifty years he hath seen, at the least, and for thirty of these he hath been an ornament to the galleys. 'Tis without doubt he was peerless in his prime. But his strength waneth not, methinks. Of a truth, to bend mightily at the oars doth exercise the whole body to increasing vigor."

"But why hast thou chained him with the chain I had thought was worn by the galleys but when in battle, lest they think to spring overboard and join the enemy, O Caius?"

"Because he hath a devil. Many devils. See him eye the knife in thy belt! He hath a madness for liberty. Three men hath he killed and yet, because he is such an oarsman as the galleys hold but once in an hundred years, his life hath been spared.

"Once he eyed the knife that Miletus the centurion wore, as he eyed thine but now. And then he sprang on him and seized it and ran swiftly, and he had wounded three men to their death ere they secured him. I know not whither he thought to flee. 'Twas impossible that he escape. He hath, as I said to thee before, O Marcus, a madness for liberty that stirreth him to wild deeds. For what he did that day he should have been given to the lions, and there were many who were urgent, even as thou wouldst have been, that he should crown the next games with his mighty death-struggles. But Festus is a soldier before all else. He decreed that the life of Dravid should be spared, because of his usefulness to the State, but that he should wear the battle cestus from that hour. In truth, no man's life would be safe in my trireme if he did not. He hath an ugly temper, and that madness for liberty which possesseth him at all times maketh him fearless of death. He would do, only Jupiter knoweth what of violence, if he had such freedom to move as these others."

"Now by the great god Pan! What thou sayest exciteth me, Caius. I would give a thousand sesterces to see him fight."

"Thou wert born a matter of twenty years too late, my Marcus. Dravid hath fought in the arena, and the sight was worth thy thousand sesterces and more. It happened in this wise. He himself got wind of the fierce desire of many to see him act the gladiator, and after a time he besought Festus without ceasing to suffer him to meet any beast they should choose in single combat, and to give him his liberty if he slew it. The youth of the city heard of his petition, and went wild, even as thou wouldst have done, O Marcus, for a sight of his prowess. So both Dravid and the young men who longed to wager their money on him continually besought Festus with such importunity that he was fain to satisfy them all. So he devised a clever trick, whereby the games were graced by the feats of this wonderful Gaul and yet the pride of the galleys was not taken from us. He granted the petition of Dravid. If he slew the beast single-handed he was to be free. But Festus cunningly stationed another where he could rush out and give, or feign to give, the final thrust. So that Dravid not having won single-handed, Festus would be guiltless in sending him back to the galleys! Also, if Dravid was too hard pressed the other gladiator was to come to his assistance. So in any case our mighty Gaul, our treasure, was to be saved to us."

"By Bacchus! I could weep, Caius, to think I was not here!"

"Thou wert not long done sucking pap, my Marcus. The games were not for such as thou wert then. And yet, I think we err in that the children are no longer brought so young to the arena."

"Torment me not, Caius. Tell me quickly what befell this Dravid."

"Oh, a splendid beast of Bengal—'twas said, a man-eater that had slain his hundreds in his own jungles—was the choice of Festus. The people when they heard it went wild with joy, to think of the magnificent Dravid pitted against that more than magnificent beast who had already slain many since he was brought hither. But Festus had the Gaul well weaponed. He greatly desired that whether he should kill the tiger or not, he should come through without a scratch and return that same day to the trireme."

"Hasten, Caius! Tell me of the struggle. Didst see it?"

"Thou art an unreasoning youth! How can I tell thee faster? Did I see it? Yea, that I did! It all fell as Festus had devised. Dravid and that Bengalese brute made the most glorious picture mine eye hath ever beheld in the arena. And he slew the beast, Marcus! He slew him without help. There was not a soul in the whole amphitheatre who did not know it was Dravid's thrust that finished him, and not the blow of the suborned gladiator who rushed up just in time to stick his knife to the hilt into the brute before he fell.

"So Dravid came back to the galleys. The very spirit of the tiger seemed to have gone into him. He knew well enough that Festus had duped him, and he looked like a crouching lion as he sat in a heap when the oars were silent brooding over it. Then he suddenly made the same petition to Festus again—canst believe?"

"I groan to think he doth not make it again, this very hour!"

"Festus knew not what to think, but at the mere whisper of seeing Dravid again there was such enthusiasm among the citizens that he consented.

"This time they chose a lion, every whit the equal of that black beast thou didst so admire—and Dravid performed the impossible with him. 'Twas a goodly sight. I would thou hadst seen it, Marcus."

"Remind me not of my loss! But tell me more fully of the fight."

"Nay, I cannot. 'Tis twenty years since.

"As before, the man Festus had appointed rushed out and thrust his sword into the staggering beast. But what think you? Dravid turned on him and made the man do battle for his life. Oh, then the people rose to him! For 'twas known to all what Festus had intended. Now by the beneficence of Jupiter, the gladiator who had been appointed to feign help to Dravid was of a noble build, and never has my blood so tingled in my veins as when they clenched. For Festus sent men quickly who seized them from behind, and two men drawing back the arms of each of them, two others took the weapons from them. Which was marvellous clever of Festus, for he desired not to stop the fight and yet he would not risk that Dravid should be wounded. So the two fought in the Gaulish manner, with naked hands. And Dravid strangled his man!"

"Ah, Jupiter!" sighed Marcus, softly.

"Then he turned in a flash to the people, and stretched out his hands; and all took his meaning. Oh, the tumult that rose! Some were for keeping him—I think they were secretly reckoning that if he returned to the galleys they might see him yet again—but most were for letting him go. My trireme all but lost its crowning star. But Festus stood firm. He sent men to lead him away without seeming violence, and caused to be circulated the report that Dravid was but kept to show his skill once more in the arena, and that quieted the people.

"But this time they reckoned without Dravid. He could never be persuaded to fight again. He sitteth ever as thou seest him now, with the look in his eyes of one who bideth his time. He looketh in vain. The liberty he craveth will be his only from the hand of Death."

"By Pluto! Thou dost touch my pity concerning this Gaul, Caius. Festus should have freed him at the demand of the people."

"Festus is too good a soldier. Look at his massive arms!"

"Whence came he?"

"I know not. From some wild tribe where he was bred up in the freedom he dreameth of night and day. It may be, a chief's son. He was taken in battle."

"Bethink you, Caius! What memories of his youth of wild freedom must be his as he sitteth in his chains!"

"I have ere now conceived that the pent-up, savage longing in his heart for the mountains of his birth doth breed the mighty strokes that are my joy. But come, thou shalt see for thyself. There is time, ere we seek the feast Glaucus spreadeth to-night in honor of thine illustrious father's son, to take thee to yon headland and return. Thou shalt see the swiftest oars Rome boasteth, my Marcus. Sit here, where thou canst mark the muscles of his mighty back."

Lo! Desire is potent.
But pray that it prove not a Fire

That shall turn, in the end, and enshroud you,
and fashion your Pyre.

CHUNDA,
WIFE OF RAM RUOY

Being
Incarnation the Fourth
of the Soul
Osru

Ram Ruoy was old, very old. Also he was rich, very rich. By an unfortunate combination of circumstances—notably the plague—Ram Ruoy's wives were all dead. But a rich old Brahmin could not cold-bloodedly be left without a wife to perform suttee for him when his time came to depart, thereby acquiring for him much salvation and a happy reincarnation when he should next be reborn. There is nothing new to the Hindoo in the idea of vicarious atonement.

So they made haste and sold to him Chunda, daughter of Dasura Mitra. There was much pomp and ceremony of marriage connected with the bargain, and large presents passed from Ram Ruoy to Mitra; wherefore the latter rejoiced greatly that his final decision eleven years before on the day of Chunda's birth had been to allow her to live. His disappointment then that she had not been a boy was bitter, and he was more than half decided during some hours to throw her into the Sacred River, with suitable prayers that the proper deity might feel duly propitiated and send a son. However the final decision had been to keep her, and now, behold! Five hundred rupees was the reward of his self-sacrifice. Truly Mitra had no cause to repent of the trouble he had put himself to, to raise her.

Chunda was well grown and pretty, and her husband was rich, very rich, and indulgent. Almost, the women who saw her jewels and silks felt envy. But not quite, for Ram Ruoy would lie on his funeral pyre before long; next moon, perhaps, or three moons hence, or ten; and Chunda would lie beside him. No, no one quite envied Chunda.

Perhaps instead, they spitefully rejoiced that her day to queen it would be short, and that they would be wearing their less costly necklaces and anklets after the smoke had risen that would make her forever indifferent to such gauds.

For there could be no glamour of doubt about Chunda's future. It was that certainty which had made necessary the costly gifts of Ram Ruoy to Dasura Mitra, who would have had to part with a goodly marriage portion to have wedded Chunda to a boy of eighteen. Dasura Mitra had taken advantage to the full of the dire necessity of Ram Ruoy, and had driven a hard bargain. It is one thing to marry off a daughter knowing that it may, perchance, become her duty to perform suttee, for there were, even at that period, widows in India. The custom of burning them all had already passed in that section. But it was quite another matter, argued Mitra, to marry her to do certain suttee for an old and otherwise wifeless man. And the price should be high. Only the malignity of the Gods, claimed Mitra, could have brought a man of Ram Ruoy's rank to such a pass that he had not a single wife left to comfort his soul on the Perilous Passage. What were five hundred rupees to a man like Ram Ruoy, when they went to purchase the boon of a wife to survive him? And indeed Ram Ruoy, when the plague had done its work and yet providentially spared him, did not haggle long over the price before he took to himself this young thing, Chunda, and breathed freely again when he thought of the future beyond the grave. Also, from a merely carnal point of view, this fresh, young, new wife pleased him. For he was old, very old, and jaded.

But there was nothing to please Chunda, except the anklets. She sometimes forgot the other things, when there were plenty of women about wondering at and desiring them. They were marvellously inlaid with gold, and at a little distance looked the all gold anklets that only a princess may wear. Some, not many, could match her other jewels, but as to anklets she stood alone.

In this other matter, alas, she stood alone also. To any wife in all Hindoostan the lot might fall to do suttee, just as any soldier may die in battle. That was bearable. But the certainty, the speedy certainty, who could look it in the face and not quail? Chunda trembled daily, nay, hourly. And the health and comfort of Ram Ruoy possessed her thoughts in the silent night watches. To keep the breath in that senile bunch of bones, ah, only to keep it there! She pushed Death from him with her strong young hands and made of herself a willing mat, lest the damp of the earth should reach his feet and work him harm.

"Delight of my eyes," said Ram Ruoy, after some six months of wedded bliss with the wife of his second childhood, "the Gods meant me no ill, as I thought in my first grief, when they took the six wives they had left me in the space of four suns. They did but plan to give me thee, that thou mightest cheer and delight my failing strength. Yea, and even hold Death from me, thou treasure! Blessed be the Gods!"

Chunda trembled.

Sometimes, in anger, Ram Ruoy reminded her of the fate stored up for her.

"Wouldst ruin me with thine itch for jewels? It is well the Gods have taken my other wives. A rajah could not buy trinkets enough to satisfy two such as thou. Thou wast an evil-liver when last on earth, without a doubt. Perchance thou didst ruin thy husband with thine extravagance, as thou dost all but ruin me, and 'tis in penance for that that thou art now set apart to burn!"

And Chunda trembled, and forgot the armlet she had been cajoling him to buy.

Others beside her husband reminded her freely of the future. There was Agra, the ugly-tempered wife of Ram Ruoy's oldest son, who ruled the women and the household.

"Thou little devil!" she would say, when no one else could hear. "Glad will I be to see thee burn! Pray Kali it be not long that I wait that much-to-be-desired sight!"

And then she would laugh and chuckle a long time, as she saw how sorely Chunda trembled.

There was much that made life a doubtful blessing to Chunda, but still she clung to it. During her honeymoon, which had been a moon of myrrh and bitterness, she had, indeed, wished herself dead, but even while she longed for death, every fibre of her healthy body shrank from *the* death that waited for her, like a karait in the grass.

It availed nothing to outshine the wives of poorer and younger men, because they, spiteful and devoid of compunction, were quick at reminding her to tremble.

"Thou'rt right to go in broidered silks, and deck thine ears with rubies," said Satartha, wife of Paryanya, with oily tongue. "Poor child! Thou hast every right to make thy life a merry one!"

And Chunda trembled.

"Beseech Krishna for a son," counseled Arthvan, her mother. "If thou dost bear him a son, then while he is yet little, thou canst implore

Ram Ruoy, and he will take another wife, lest, perchance, the manling suffer from thy loss. Of a surety, when thou wert last earth-born thou didst some grievous wrong, that the angry Gods should have marked thee out for this long torment of fear."

But Chunda was a barren woman. Not even a useless woman-babe came to mock her. Ram Ruoy was old, very old, and she invoked the intervention of Krishna in vain. One by one she went to every shrine she could persuade her husband to let her visit.

After these pilgrimages there was always the sick fear, as she drew near home, lest they sat within and waited her coming that they might shave her head. Many nights she woke and felt of her hair with terrified haste. Sometimes she dreamed that she put up her hand and her beautiful silky hair was not—sign of the near approach of her ordeal.

The very worst of all was to watch the funeral pyres of other men, men invariably younger than her husband. They could not, in fact, well be older. Sometimes the widows who burned with them were younger than she, but that counted for little. They had been happy wives until—she counted the days that each had known that the death of her lord was certain.

They had not been bought for this. Sometimes she knew they loved their husbands and gladly paid the price that secured to them future happiness. There was Misra, now. Her beloved had been young and strong and beautiful, until the night he had drowsily sought to free himself from the weight of the cobra that had coiled on his smooth, bare breast. Never had the thought come to Misra that she was to burn beside him in her one and twentieth year. Chunda felt that she could have borne to be Misra.

"Desire of my heart," said Ram Ruoy with clumsy playfulness, as they returned from witnessing her suttee, "see thou tend me softly that the day when thou shalt follow Misra, and climb the steps to me, be kept far from us."

And Chunda trembled.

That night she woke, screaming. She had climbed the steps; she had lain down beside the corpse of Ram Ruoy; she had felt the fire. The pain of the burning woke her, and she lay and trembled till daybreak. After that the dream came often. Twice, thrice in a moon, she climbed the steps and the flames lapped her flesh.

Still Ram Ruoy did not die. The breath was yet in him and he doddered about, calling Chunda his little Gift of Life and chuckling that he was the Beloved of the Gods, since when he had thought to die they had given him a beautiful bride and ten more years than he had hoped to enjoy.

Chunda was three and twenty when they did at last cut off her beautiful hair. For twelve full years Ram Ruoy kept the breath in his shrunken frame—though two score sunsets seemed more than he was like to see, on the day he made little Chunda his wife lest he fail of a widow.

That night she half woke and her hand crept drowsily up to her head that she might take comfort in the feel of her soft hair. Then the air was torn with screams, for the horrible prickliness of a shorn scalp was under her shaking fingers, and the truth she had been too dazed to realize before came home.

The chief priests counseled her. A widow must mount beside her husband of her own free will, yet it was an unheard of thing for an only wife to refuse. They labored with her, pointing out that there was but one path appointed for her by the gods. They made her drunk with soma and wrought upon her over-strung nerves till they wrung from her a loath consent. Then they sent her home.

That night the dream came again and she woke, raving. But no one, though she threw herself on her face before each, turned a listening ear to her refusal to lie beside Ram Ruoy. To the high priest she had given consent. Therefore she could be bound and dragged there. They told her so.

They drugged her at last, because she continued to fill the house with her shrieks and disturb their slumbers. But they could not risk killing her—that would not acquire merit for Ram Ruoy—and the biggest dose they dared give only partly quieted her. Sometimes she lay in a waking dream, living over the coming hour. Sometimes she shrieked without ceasing and sometimes she raved that she cared nought for the future happiness of Ram Ruoy and would not go.

She struck at Chitiji, the high priest; but what punishment is commanded for a widow about to immolate herself for the repose of her husband's soul?

To Agra she screamed:

"Thou shalt return to earth and burn a widow, because thou art glad I go to the bier of Ram Ruoy. All—all of you—" the sweep of her arm included the priests, "shall suffer because of this. It may be that for the sins of a former birth this thing has come upon me, but in your future lives it shall be counted to you as sin that ye force me against my will to climb the steps to Ram Ruoy. Yea, it shall be counted to you as sin!" She threw herself back in a convulsion. A very little more and Ram Ruoy might have been cheated of his rights.

Freshly stupefied with drugs she climbed the steps, supported and held close prisoner by two of her husband's sons. But at sight of Ram Ruoy's sheeted figure she broke from them and fled, and fought them with the strength of madness as they dragged her back.

The women looked on with horror at the shame she put upon their sex and called out to the sons of Ram Ruoy to bind her with cords, lest the worthless one rob Ram Ruoy of his sacred dues.

The flames lapped her flesh, as they had in her dreams, but she could not wake.

Lo! Desire is potent.
But Justice abides, overruling.

And Desire, being spent, bends the neck to
her rod and her schooling.

LOVIS,
SIEUR LE BRENT

Being
Incarnation the Fifth
of the Soul
Osru

To be thrust into a dungeon was no figure of speech in the days when the Norman barons were building up their power, cementing it securely with violence. They took you by the shoulders in those times and thrust you brutally into the darkness, so that you stumbled forward drunkenly, and except the cell was narrow and you brought up against the opposite wall suddenly, you lost your balance and came to earth sprawling on your face. And as you lay there partly stunned, you heard the great key creak and the receding footsteps of the gaoler as he went back to the light of heaven and the sight of the blue sky.

'Twas a fearsome thing to offend one of those lawless autocrats of Normandy, with none to question his decrees or bring him to book for injustice. Men went into his ample prisons striplings and came out, feet foremost, cadaverous gray-beards; having been forgotten while my lord pursued his enemies and equally forgotten while he pursued his pleasures.

Lovis, Sieur le Brent, picked himself up and strode around close to the walls of the foul, damp place into which he had just been thrust, like one demented. He made the circuit some hundred times perhaps, before thought came back to him. For the mixture of daze and fear and mad desire to take some one by the throat that filled him when he first found himself in the dungeon of the man he served with his sword, was a far cry from thinking. But in time his brain cleared, and while his body continued to sweep on with the tireless strides of a coursing hound his brain began to race still more swiftly, seeking out the chances of speedy release.

"Now God be thanked that I have no store of land or gold. When did I think to be glad that I had nought in the world beyond my sword? 'Twould be with me even as with poor Gibert de Rohan, God rest him in Heaven, and 'twas for less than mine offense that he was first thrust—perchance into this very hole."

Lovis le Brent's blood chilled at the fancy that the luckless Sieur de Rohan might have spent his brief imprisonment restlessly measuring these very walls, even as he was now measuring them. It weighed on him heavily as an evil omen that almost his first coherent thought in this place had been of de Rohan.

"But de Rohan had estates which would tempt a king's anger to wax instead of waning with time, as is nature. He had never a chance, once he gave de Breouille cause to seize him."

This same de Breouille, who had been tempted beyond his power to resist by de Rohan's wealth, (albeit he imprisoned him in anger and without any ulterior idea of confiscating his worldly goods), was now the active and at present triumphing enemy of le Brent.

"My chances are good, so help me God," said le Brent. He put away from him resolutely the thought of the life-long prisoners in that very set of dungeons. Prisoners whose histories he had known, whose histories every one knew, but in whose behalf no one lifted a finger lest they should suddenly depart from the haunts of their fellows and join them. Instead he thought over the stories of every prisoner of de Breouille's who had been released or had escaped. The list was long enough to be encouraging.

"If all else fail, there are ofttimes gaolers—I must study these varlets here—" Prison had not yet changed the Sieur's attitude toward the common herd.

"But after all's said, my best chance is that de Breouille's whim against me will die out, mayhap in a few days. If the damsel for whose sweet sake I am here would but bestir herself in my behalf—yea, if she should grant de Breouille his uttermost desire, and but demand in return banishment for me,—I ask no more than banishment,—how gladly would I give her up! For I must give her up, in all case, if so be he keep me here.

"There is much to be tried. By God's help, I shall not miss the sight of many suns—"

Ten years.

Lovis le Brent beat his head against the wall. Another will-o-the-wisp hope had that day gone. But there was still a chance. Lovis le Brent's pluck would not altogether down. There was always the chance that the Baron's whim would change. He had lain down and risen up by the light of that hope for near four thousand days. But to-day it shone very dimly. Lovis tore his hair. Despair all but possessed him. He beat his fists against the wall. It was not possible, at that moment, to feel that the Baron's whim would change.

The fact was, his whim was gone. He had merely forgotten. There were men, prisoners for fifty years in that same castle gaol, put there by the Baron's grandfather for trifling offences and simply left there by his successors. Le Brent knew this. Every one knew it. But no one cared. And every one knew that he, Lovis le Brent, was unjustly detained, deprived of his liberty, but no one cared. He beat with his two hands upon his breast until he fell exhausted.

Twenty years.

There was still one chance.

The Baron would without doubt die first, and then he would raise heaven and earth to reach the ear of his successor. De Breouille had to his credit fifty ill-spent years, le Brent was ten years younger. Also, de Breouille was always fighting with his neighbors. He might at any time be killed. A just God grant it soon. And it sometimes happened, too, that a new Baron set free the men who cumbered the dungeons he would presently fill himself.

Lovis threw himself on the filthy straw and lay

there a while in a semi-stupor. Hope deferred maketh the heart sick—and the brain sick, too.

Presently a frenzy took him and he leaped up, his eyes gleaming. Swinging his arms like mad he tore around the dark place and jumped and leaped and shrieked aloud. No gaoler came to quiet him for no one heard.

When he was tired out he threw himself on the straw again and slept.

Thirty years.

His hair is white, but his body is still rugged. His mad orgies of violent rage have served as exercise and kept him strong.

There is a new hope.

The Baron is at war with a mightier Baron. If he loses—God send he may—he loses all, and the new Baron will very surely set his prisoners free. Out of scorn for his conquered enemy, he will certainly do it.

Gaolers are fear-smitten creatures not easy to bribe to a righteous deed, lest their hides pay the price, or lest they find themselves behind the key they have so often turned. Belike, also, the bribes at le Brent's command are not ample enough to tempt most of the brotherhood. But every new gaoler is always a new chance. It may be that, some day, one braver than the rest will wink at the escape of a prisoner who has not been inquired after for fifteen years.

Forty years.

The Baron is not dead. Not he, but the Baron he fought some ten years since went to the wall.

But it must come soon now, it *must* come. He cannot live forever, with the devil waiting hungrily for his wicked soul.

Lovis le Brent sits much with his head on his hands. His strength is going for the old rages take hold of him less often. But his head is clear and strong. He has never ceased to calculate the chances left him.

Fifty years.

De Breouille is just dead. But le Brent's dungeon has another occupant.

It fell empty these two years since, when Lovis le Brent almost beat his brains out against the floor—at last. Although he did not quite beat them out yet he addled them finally, and shortly thereafter he left the dungeon.

For dungeons are places for the living, not the dead.

Lo! Desire is potent.
She twists you a rope for your using.

But mayhap they will hang you, ere night,
with that rope of your choosing.

DON JOSE DE RODERIGUEZ

Being
Incarnation the Sixth
of the Soul
Osru

Don Jose de Roderiguez was in the clutches of The Three. The torments of the Inquisition were closing in around him. How and why it had come to pass he had but a dazed notion. He fed and housed two merchants from Cadiz, who sought his hospitality on a certain eve of Ascension. That was all. And because of that simple act of kindness all this trouble and terror had come upon him. Was there no justice in Heaven? Was God Himself dead, that He had not heard his hourly cries for help these two years past?

Don Jose de Roderiguez was already more than half crazed. Only a lumpishly unimaginative creature, with almost undifferentiated brains, could lie long in the dungeons of The Three and keep those brains unclouded.

"Christ witnesseth! It might as easily have been any other man in the market place as my thrice-wretched self, my father!"

He beat his breast and raised to his lips the hempen rope that bound the robe of the padre, stammering out to his patient ears for the hundredth time the story of his misfortunes.

"They offered me excellent golden doubloons for a night's lodging. A curse on their money! And then it comes to light they are heretics—God knoweth I wotted not nor dreamed it, else had I delivered them up with my own hands—and shortly thereafter I am haled before The Three for the heinous crime of harboring heretics; the rest thou knowest. By the Holy Virgin Mary, the Blessed Mother of Our Sacred Lord, I am no heretic. Why will not The Three believe? I have bared my thoughts to them from the hour of my birth."

He had indeed. Don Jose de Roderiguez groaned and smote his forehead as he remembered the ordeal. Once only, shortly after his arrest, he had faced The Three. For five maddening hours he stood in an ague of fear and answered their entrapping questions—from whose entangling meshes but four in Seville had ever escaped. This cell of his had seemed a place of peace and refuge ever since. But at any moment Their summons might come.

Don Jose wept weakly. He was no longer the

brawling, dare-devil braggart who had looked up boldly at the sun that beat on Seville for some thirty odd years. It was many months since that gruesome interview, but he dreaded the next so much that he would have instantly chosen life-long imprisonment, in the peace and comparative plenty and freedom from physical pain that were now his, rather than face The Three again.

"Holy father, no man in Seville hath lived farther from heresy than wretched Jose de Roderiguez. I call all the saints in Heaven to witness how terrible is the injustice under which I suffer. Since my pious mother took me to mass at five years old, till now, in my forty-first year, I have not wavered in obedience to the Church. However great my sins, God knoweth I have always confessed them and patiently performed the penances, howsoever severe. Never have I complained. 'Tis true that in the matter of the girl Manuela, whereof I told thee something formerly, the holy father certainly did fleece me somewhat, but God is my witness, it never entered into the heart of de Roderiguez to complain. I was but too glad to appease God for my sins——"

The friar's countenance changed.

"Thou sayest a priest of the Most Blessed Jesus robbed thee?"

The words rang coldly—and loudly. There were those listening behind the innocent grating high in the wall on the inner side of the room. The holy father feared lest they had missed this point of his mumbling penitent's confession.

A priest may not repeat outside the secrets of the confessional, but if, by chance, they are overheard——

De Roderiguez clutched his throat.

"Shrive me! shrive me, father! I am as one

drunken with anguish. I say what I do not mean. Thou wilt not tell The Three?"

"Fear not, my son. My lips are sealed. Thou knowest full well a priest tells nothing—nothing. He stands between thee and thy God, not between thee and man. But this is a grievous thing, son, a very grievous thing. In the eyes of God thou art sorely guilty. Then what matters it how it appeareth in the eyes of men? Thou saidst thy confessor robbed thee, and I trow he did but set thee a fitting penance for a deadly sin. If The Three heard thee,—nay, nay, *I* will not tell them—but if The Three did hear thee utter such blasphemy against the Holy Mother Church, methinks thou wouldst have short shrift!"

"I meant it not," moaned de Roderiguez. "I knew not what I said. I am stupid from sleepless nights and wretched days. It is now nearing two years that no one hath come nigh me, saving thee." 'Twas the habit of The Three to wear out the stubborn ones, whose stories could in no wise be shaken, by means of these long, terrifying silences. "The august Three have forgotten the miserable de Roderiguez."

"Not so," said the friar, significantly. "Thou shalt shortly find The Three have had thee in remembrance these past two years. And as for this damning thing that thou hast said, the evil in men's hearts will out. Drunken men speak truth, and thou wast indeed as one drunk and unguarded in thy speech by reason of thy sleepless vigils. But I will shrive thee, my son. Thou shalt lie all night face downward on this stone floor, fasting and without drink, from the hour the gaoler visits thee till he come again with to-morrow's sun. And thou shalt tell thy beads without ceasing. And further, because thou hast said a priest robbed thee—perchance thou hadst best make voluntary offering to the

Church in fitting restitution, seest thou, for that thou hast slandered the Lord thy God through his earthly vicar. I leave to thee what portion of thy worldly goods thou wilt bestow. The Church is ever needy, and thy sin is great. And the Lord loveth the cheerful gift."

"I will, father," whispered the now deeply terrified cavalier.

The priest withdrew, his task at last accomplished. Weekly for two and twenty months he had been confessing de Roderiguez and seeking to gain his confidence, in the service of The Three. To-day, for the first time, de Roderiguez had let fall a word that could be used against him. The evil in the heart will out.

The friar sighed. There could now be no doubt that the unhappy man was a heretic and a harborer of heretics. The Blessed Lord had graciously decreed that he should have a goodly heritage of land and gold, which would henceforth be held in trust for the poor by the Holy Church. 'Twas indeed needless that Don Jose should present it, or any portion thereof, of his own free will as a sin offering. His conviction as a heretic would now follow without possibility of failure, and both his life and his estates would be forfeit.

The friar paused to sigh again over the depravity of human hearts. Then his thoughts reverted to Don Jose's fortune and the penitential gift he meant he should make to Holy Mother Church. He studied long and earnestly on how he should move him to give up all. The friar was an artistic man in his professional capacity. The Church could rise in her might and take, but 'twere far more seemly that the don himself should give in grief and penitence, than that the Church, however justly, should seize. Moreover, 'twere better for the poor wretch's soul that he, ignorant that these worldly possessions were in fact no longer his, should yield them up in submissive penitence and accept the cross of poverty for his terrible sin. Also, was it not a covetous desire for the doubloons of the heretics that had first led him astray?

The friar pondered long and earnestly, telling his beads the while. Finally he drew a breath of relief and satisfaction and went to vespers. Don Jose would, without doubt, be moved ere long to make a princely gift to the Church, a full and free surrender of his earthly all.

But de Roderiguez, though sleepless, did not lie in penance on the floor of his cell saying his prayers that night. Before the hour the holy father had set all thought of prayers and penance was wiped from his mind as fire wipes the impression of the signet ring from wax.

Toward nightfall de Roderiguez had another guest, who muffled his face from the gaoler, but showed it when they were alone to the prisoner. He spoke briefly, and his stay was short. But that brief stay was sufficient to complete the work of The Three in remodeling to madness the brain of Jose.

" 'Tis twenty years, Jose de Roderiguez. Dost remember?"

De Roderiguez remembered. So well that he instinctively stood at bay. Some of the brute courage natural to the man, that The Three had all but sweated out of him with the sweat of fear, returned.

"Thou hast had thy day. Now mine! Thy greater wealth did get thee the wife of my desire. For fifteen years I suffered in mind and body because of that. Thy kinsmen were many, else had I slain thee ere now. But all ends well. Thou art singled out by The Three. Know, 'twas I that caused the report that the strangers from Cadiz who sojourned at thy house were heretics. Ah! Dios! Long did I wait to draw thee into the net of The Three! But Mary the Blessed Virgin at length heard my prayers. This day thou hast signed the warrant of thy death. Spies of The Three lurked behind yon grating and heard what thou didst tell thy priest."

The knees of Jose de Roderiguez bent. He caught at the grating of the little window to straighten them and clung there. But he still faced his guest defiantly.

"I have gained the ear of one of The Three, at great cost, and asked for thee a boon. I have asked for thee, that ere thou diest thou shouldst know the embraces of the Iron Maiden. He hath said it. He will not fail. 'Tis my estate in Granada assures to me this boon I have asked for thee. Think of me, de Roderiguez, thou base-born whelp of a devil, when the Iron Maiden folds thee softly, softly."

De Roderiguez drew himself up a little straighter with the remnant of his strength, still clinging to the grating.

His guest continued.

"This one thing more I asked for thee. Rest easy in thy heart. Thou shalt be spared the death of a heretic. Thou shalt not burn. He hath promised it. And I have such a palace in Granada as would move a prince to keep his promises. Nay, verily, thou shalt not burn. Thou shalt not come alive from the arms of the Maiden. The day is even now set for thy bridal. I will tell thee no more than that 'tis that same Saint's Day whereon thou madest thine the bride I burned for twenty years ago. Had Death not snatched her from thee, that would I now do. Whether thy nuptials with the Iron Maid shall come to pass within this year, thou shalt not know. The Three move slowly. How long already hast thou lain here? But surely, surely, she awaits thee to be thy bride. I would thou hadst had no other! Dost feel her soft kisses on thine eyes, de Roderiguez? I see thou dost! Not once, but many times she shall embrace thee, and thou shalt die in agony.

"Adios, Jose de Roderiguez!"

Lo! Desire is potent.
Mayhap you will find it has knotted

A scourge for your quivering flesh.
Whereof only God wotted.

HAFID
THE DWARF

Being
Incarnation the Seventh
of the Soul
Osru

Baron von Altenberg, crusader, came home to his castle on the Rhine and his little daughter Berta from dealings with the Saracens. He had given the infidel dogs many goodly blows and, by the grace of God, brought home a whole skin. Also, he had fetched with him among the spoils of his right arm a certain manikin of a kind seldom seen in Teuton lands. This manikin was a present for the little Berta.

"Hi! little maid," quoth the Baron, "I have brought thee a goodly toy. Behold!" and he pulled forward the little man who came barely to the elbow of the fourteen-year-old Berta.

"So. Thou shalt have some one to keep thee merry, when next I go to wrest the tomb of our Blessed Lord from the accursed hands of the Turks. He hath frolicsome antics shall make thee laugh till thy sides are sore. And he hath a clever wit. Already he knoweth our tongue as his own. He is thine, Bertlein. And thou shalt teach him to love the Savior and hate the Saracen. Belike, thou wilt find thou hast little to teach him concerning that last. Methinks he hath good reason to hate the Saracen. Look thou here."

He laid hold of the dwarf and pulled him toward him, not roughly but without taking account of his manhood or even his humanity; rather, treating him as something between a child and a doll. He stripped off the short Turkish jacket he wore and jerked open the blouse shirt underneath.

Across his chest, laid evenly with an awful precision that suggested a devilish skill in wielding the whip, were the scars of great welts that had once gone deep.

The sensitive Berta's impressions of her new toy and playmate were scarcely as roseate as her father had expected. Later Northern Europe learned the dreadful art of making dwarfs, but at this period they were unknown. Hafid's squat, barrel-shaped trunk and hands that touched the floor like an ape's moved her to something like nausea, but the scars on his breast and a certain wistfulness in his smile stirred the depths of her gentle heart. She put out a timid hand and the dwarf, skilled beyond more fortunate men in reading faces, sank thankfully to his knees and kissed the fingers of his new mistress, aware that a happier era had begun for him.

As for Berta, she found her father had by no means overstated Hafid's power to amuse. But none of his tricks and antics so absorbed and fascinated her as the tales he told of the people among whom he had lived. Weird tales, as though the Arabian Nights folk (of whom she had never heard) had come to life and frolicked anew.

"But tell me thine own tale, Hafid!"

"Nay, mistress!"

"Then will I have thee beaten!"

"Nay, mistress! But tell me rather of the blessed Savior. Thou'rt over young to hear the tale of Hafid the dwarf, fair mistress!"

"Hafid! Then I shall assuredly have thee beaten if thou dost continue to disobey me!"

But Hafid only smiled wistfully and renewed

his request to be told of the Holy Jesus. He knew well 'twas not through such lips as the tender-hearted Berta's that commands for beatings came.

Because Berta asked him very often to tell what had befallen himself, it happened that he heard very often the story of Christ. So good came of it. For presently the wondrous gentleness of the Holy One of Nazareth crept into his heart and drove out the bitterness that man's inhumanity had put there, and at last he could speak to Berta quietly and without rancor of those things that had been his lot.

"I am a Greek. The Turks stole me, little maid. This, our blessed Lord permitted. Mayhap had I known Him then He had not suffered it. While my bones were still soft and young they misshaped me thus. Nay, the good Lord gave me not this body. 'Tis the work of human hands. I am thy plaything, little lady, but to be *thy* plaything is to be free and to be a man. Yea, a man! To be the plaything of Ahmed the sheikh—ah, blessed Jesus, let me forget!

"The pirates who stole me kept me eight years and taught me many things. For a dwarf must be skilled to amuse if he thinks to keep his skin on his bones.

"At what, methinks, must have been sixteen years, though I know not for certain mine age when they snatched me from Greece, they sold me to Ahmed and that black devil of a Saracen owned my body and soul till thy father took me from him. Of a truth, the dear Lord Jesus looked with pity on me then.

" 'Twas not that sometimes he beat me till all went dark and I fell. Men are beaten. Stripes I can take like a man, for I am strong. If I had nought to remember save those times when I was beaten to unconsciousness 'twere a light matter. That I could forgive, even as our blessed

Lord commandeth. But the cursed Ahmed had a cruel wit and tormented me sorely. 'Twas his whim to have me led about like a bear by a collar and chain, and with me a brown bear, smallish and of a rough coat. What the beast did I must do, and all a bear's tricks I learned. Did it dance,—I danced too. Like a bear, cumbrously. When it went on all fours, I also must go on all fours. 'Twas bitter! To be mishandled thus and treated as a beast to make men sport!

"Ahmed held us his choicest entertainment and had us out to liven all his guests. Each of us had a keeper, a huge black-a-moor, the twain dressed in the self-same fashion. For the bear, 'twas nought. He had not a man's feelings wherewith to suffer at the indignities put upon us.

"In an evil hour Ahmed, wearying of using me as a dancing bear, bethought him to get a monkey and train me to monkey capers. So I must needs learn to swing on bars and hang head downward and such like tricks. 'Twas worse than death. What the ape did I must copy when 'twas Ahmed's caprice thus to make sport of me, to while the time. And when the animal swung by the tail they would grow unseemly with laughter. I could not follow. Forsooth, he was the cleverer.

"These be but the worst of the ways Ahmed hath devised from time to time to torment me. May the blessed Lord put out his eyes and wither his arms!

"I will confess the truth to thee now, sweet mistress! Hafid hath hitherto feared to tell thee this, lest thou shouldst desire to do likewise!

"Nay, nay! I know it well! Thou wouldst not! If the Blessed Lord is gentle, even as thou, then will I, too, love Him forever."

Lo! Desire is potent.
Behold in the Sheaves you are reaping
The Harvest of Former Desire.
So a truce to your weeping.

JEANIE CAMPBELL

Being
Incarnation the Eighth
of the Soul
Osru

The London alleys were dark and far from safe in the days of Bess the Queen. This one, however, held nothing worse than a bedraggled girl. She crept out of a doorway and clasped the arms of the men who passed. But they shook her off. She was not of those who create desire. Consumption was wasting her to the bone.

Close on to midnight came another pedestrian, the first for half an hour.

"Come wi' me, man dear. Come awa' wi' me," she wheedled, with strained coquetry.

The man essayed to free himself from her clinging but less roughly than the others had. She was not to be so lightly shaken off. She plead with him eagerly.

"Not I, lass. Gang hame alang and let be thy de'il's trade for this one night, i' the name o' God."

He thrust his hand into his pocket for the coin which should free her from the necessity of keeping longer vigil on the doorstep.

He found the girl's hand there.

"Sae, sae, lass?" said Duncan McDonald. He drew out the interloping hand and looked at it. The frail, damp fingers still held the half crown they had closed over.

The girl began to laugh hysterically.

"At last! at last!" she said, over and over, mixing the words with the laughter. "At last! at last! at last!"

The laugh twisted itself into a cough that shook her till she would have fallen if McDonald had not caught her. He drew her down on the steps of the nearest house and put his brandy flask to her lips.

"Now, lass," he said sternly, when it became possible to speak to her again, "tell me a'. I canna leave thee here to pick the gowd frae the pockets o' the night wanderers. The Lord kens weel 'tis nae waur than thy trade, but the law suffers the tane, an' punishes the tither. Come, lassie, come." The girl was sobbing convulsively.

"I dinna care what ye do wi' me," was all she would say. "I kent it maun come tae this." The forlorn droop of her shoulders smote Duncan. He drew her into the bar of moonlight that was the sole lamp of that hole of darkness.

"Tut, tut," he muttered. "Bitter business! unco

bitter business! Here, lass." He pressed into her hand the piece of money he had taken from her inert fingers and another with it. "Tak' them. The gowd is naught. Now gie o'er greetin' an' tell me a'."

The girl bent forward and strained to see his face.

"Art a man o' God, guidman?" she whispered. She had noted the clerical cut of his garments when he drew her to the light.

"Aye, by the grace o' Christ, wha' bade the Magdalen gang free an' sin nae mair. Tell me thy tale. Thou'rt sick unto death, an' yet thou'rt fain to sell thy body to the de'il. Aye, an' this ither matter o' the gowd. Ye ken weel the penalty o' the law for sic as ye caught stealing. Nae, be na fearfu' o' me, but tell me a'. An' see," the sternness crept into his voice again, "see thou tell't me true."

The girl sobbed quietly.

"I sell mysel whiles I am beaten an' driven

forth tae get gowd. Look!" She pulled the dress off her shoulder, indifferently, turning slightly to show her bruised back.

Duncan let slip a groan at what he saw.

"For twal nights I hae taen the siller, whiles nae man wad tak up wi' me, an I daurna gang back wi' out gowd—I daurna! Jock is cruel! The river is the place for me, syne men winna look at me nae mair. Lang syne the river's waited for me. For a' my kind it waits. I hae tried an' tried, but I canna do it. Somewhat aye hauds me back wi' a strang arm. The water is sae black an' cauld it frights me. 'Tis like throwing yoursel' into the mou' o' the pit o' hell. 'Tis strange, but I fear death waur than I fear Jock. An' I kenna why. I kenna why! For Jock is the very de'il himsel. I maun get the courage to seek out the river some day—gin Jock doesna beat me dead first. Or I dinna hang for stealing. Gae ye tae hae me hang, man o' God?"

"Nae, nae, lass," said McDonald, hastily, fearing another paroxysm of hysteria. "Didna I gie thee the gowd? Hae peace. Ye shanna hang. Nor throw thysel into the river. God forgie all men! An' the brute ye ca' Jock shanna beat ye mair. Ye maun die, puir lass. The seal o' death is e'en now upo' thee. Canna ye see it yoursel? But ye shall hae peace an' a saft bed, an' lo'eing care, and ye shall learn o' thy lo'eing Savior, wha has bled an' died for sic as thee. Wilt come wi' me, lass? I'll hide thee sae thou'lt nae mair see this Jock, wham God will punish in his ain guid time. Ah!" For the girl had quietly lost consciousness. Until he felt her heart McDonald feared she was dead.

"Hae ye heard?" said old Margaret Morrison to Peg Nicholson, her crony. "Campbell's Jeanie cam hame last night. Lord God! Ye maun see her! Her that waur syne sic a bonnie lassie, she's nae mair than skin stretched o'er banes. The puir, white face o' her!

"Aye, ye kent? 'Twas Meester McDonald, o' Alexander's kirk on the ither side o' Ayr, that found the puir lass at the de'il's wark i' the Lunnon streets.

"Wi' Lady Mary Beaton she maun gang tae Lunnon town seven years syne. I kent her weel, the sonsie lass. 'Twas by some English de'il o' ae sarving man she was undone. Nae, na sae as ye think. Her heart didna stray. She lo'ed him not, then or ever. He kidnappit her. She was snatched frae the end o' the garden o' my Lady Mary's, an' keepit close prisoner, wi'in lockit rooms. This cursed English lackey kent a great laird had cast eyes o' luve on Jeanie, but Jeanie wadna hae him. Sae this Jock, this black-hearted spawn o' the midden, thought tae get her, an' bargain wi' the great man for her. An' sae he did. God maun set him i' the middle o' the Pit, for what he has done tae her. Hey, tutti taiti! He made her suffer!

"Syne cam ither lairds an' gentles, an' Jock bade them come in. But he wadna let Jeanie gang out, till the great lairds wanted her nae mair, an' the cough had grippit her. *Then* he sent her into the street. Puir pretty Jeanie! Puir sonsie lassie! An' guid as she waur bonnie. Why has the Lord dealt sae heavily wi' sic an ane?"

"An' we hae thought lang syne 'twas by her ain evil wish that nane kent what had come tae her. An' her mither wi' breakin' heart! I dinna ken why the Lord has done it a'!"

"Meester McDonald bides i' the village tae labor for her soul. A guid man. God hae him i' his keeping!"

Jeanie shook her head.

"I winna believe there's a God—or in Christ, His Son," she said.

"My lass, my lass, dinna blaspheme!" cried Duncan, the sweat of anguish starting out on his forehead. "Dinna tempt the Lord thy God, wha is able an' willin' tae save thy soul alive by th' bluid o' His dear Son."

But Jeanie still shook her head. Her eyes burned.

"I hae thought o' it night an' day. There canna be a God. Ye, wha are but a man, wad ye hae delivered me into the hands o' Jock? Gin God were God, an' nae a de'il, wad He do waur than ye wad do? What hae I e'er done, that wicked men suld harm me? There wasna ane I didna shrink frae. Nae ane. 'Twas always violence. Ilka day an' ilka, ilka night. An' ye tauld me God is Luve! Whar was He, in His might, when I had need o' Him?"

"His ways are na sic as our ways," said Duncan, helplessly. "Wha are we, tae judge Him? Ye dinna ken what secret sin maun be in your heart, lass. Man canna ken the ways o' the Lord. They are righteous."

"Nae. Man canna ken sic ways," said Jeanie, scornfully.

"Repent," pleaded Duncan. "Ye daurna die in your sins, an' gang tae Hell."

"My sins?" cried Jeanie, her voice shrilling suddenly. "Wha sinned, me or Jock? He beat me syne I maun gang out an' fetch him gowd. Was that the justice o' God or His mighty luve? Tell me that, man o' God!"

"Wae's me! Ye'll gang tae Hell. I canna save ye!" groaned McDonald, burying his face in his hands.

Jeanie put out a frail hand and touched his shoulder.

"I hae been in Hell," she said. "When I was young an' innocent He pit me there. He maun do as He chooses wi' me now. I canna believe that He is guid."

She turned her face wearily to the wall. McDonald knelt suddenly.

"Oh, thou great an' just God, save the soul o' this puir bairn o' Thine." In his agony, he said the same words over and over blindly. His power to pray coherently deserted him but an aching desire burned in every fibre of him that this so wronged child should reach Heaven.

Afterward he never could remember how long he stammered out his heart-broken petition, or say whether Jeanie waked or slept. He could not even tell them whether he continued to utter aloud the prayer that filled his heart. But presently Jeanie clutched his arm and cried out so sharply that he looked up startled.

Jeanie sat straight up—Jeanie, who had not lifted her head for days—staring not at but beside him.

Her eyes were raised to about the height of a man's head but McDonald could not see what she saw. Yet he knew. Yes, he knew! As he watched her face change from wonder to awe, and from awe to peace, and from peace to love, he knew whose face she saw with the inner vision and whose voice she listened to. It was no surprise to him when she whispered, "Aye, Lord!" The smile that came to her mouth at that moment did not fade when she presently dropped back limply. It was still there when she lay in her shroud and witnessed silently for him as he told his unbelievable story of the goodness and compassion of Christ.

Lo! Desire is potent.
So weaponed, you will not be beaten.

But the Fruits of Desire, whether Honey or Gall, must be eaten.

JACKSON'S MILLIE

Being
Incarnation the Ninth
of the Soul
Osru

Another julep? You'll find nothing like that, sir, in the length and breadth of New England. Yes, sir. I'm a yankee. Connecticut yankee. I don't have this here southern accent because I wa'n't brought up by a nigger mammy. That's how they get it. I reckon you know that. The southerners ought to be ashamed of themselves, talking like niggers. I've hung onto my r's for forty years and I don't expect ever to lose them. And I've got a yankee nurse for the youngster to keep his English pure. He gets lammed every time he says "heah." I won't have it. I had the best schooling the north has to give, and he's going to have the same. Harvard '77, sir. No, I wasn't with Washington. It didn't matter to *me* what the government was just so it got stable again, so I took it quietly and got an education and let those that wanted to, fight it out. The best way when you have nothing at stake yourself.

It's altogether a matter of business with me, living in Mississippi. I'm not here because I like their damn climate, but to breed niggers. Oh, I raise cotton, too, but that isn't the main crop. Got to have something to keep their dirty black hands busy on. My real business since I turned twenty-five has been to breed slaves for the market. I saw the future of cotton way back in

1780. Yes, sir; predicted then that blacks would drop out of use naturally in the north. There wa'n't anything they could do better, or half as well, as whites. But I saw the south would need 'em, need 'em bad. I said to myself that the kind bred on the soil would be like gold among brass, beside the trash picked up at random by the slavers off the African coast and packed so thick in the hold they were more dead than alive when they got them on the block. And I wa'n't far wrong. I underestimated it a little.

I don't know any one else who's had the sense to go about it systematically and scientifically, as I have. I breed 'em, I tell you, breed 'em like cattle. That's what they are, a high grade domestic animal. I count on a brat a year from the gals. Oh, no, that's not unreasonable. Why, they come mighty near that left to themselves. You don't understand niggers. You northerners never do.

You see that's pretty much all the work I expect of them. I won't allow the women to pull cotton. They're all house niggers, and the Lord Almighty knows they have a pretty easy time of it. No, of course there'd be nothing in it if everybody bred for the market, but as it is, my stock is known all over the south and I'm offered higher prices every year. You see I won't keep a man on the place that isn't fancy breed, so to speak. Sound of wind and limb and strong as an ox.

No, sir, I am *not* troubled with sentimental feelings when it comes to separating mothers and children! That's all bosh. You northerners don't understand niggers and you never will. You picture them to yourselves with "white" feelings, but that's not so. Any way the Lord separates parents and children every day and no one expects Him to stop. When I sell a likely youngster down the river all his dam has to do is to imagine that he died and be resigned. And that's what I tell her if she goes to make a fuss. He has died, as far as she's concerned. "The Lord gave, and the Lord hath taken away. Blessed be the name of the Lord." That's her cue.

Oh, I've eliminated the question of fathers from the problem altogether. Couldn't be bothered. I simply will not let the wenches marry. If the men want to marry on other plantations I don't object, but they're satisfied on the whole with my way. I tell you again, as I told you before, they don't know anything about the "white" point of view.

I've got my neighbors down on me, because I won't let the gals marry. But what's the odds? It's the same thing in Dutch, their way and mine. Take my neighbor on the next plantation now, Godfrey Carter, Col. Godfrey Carter. Half his pickaninnies are a damn sight lighter than the color of the wenches and their lawful wedded husbands justifies. When you breed for the market, as I do, some few rules are necessary. And I notice that they buy my niggers just the same, even if they do slander my methods.

But it doesn't fall very hard on the women, to part with their offspring, as a general thing. Usually the brats are at least half grown before I have an offer I'll look at and then, as I tell the wenches when they offer to take it nasty once in a while—they've always plenty more—and plenty to come.

I've never had any real trouble, except with Millie. Millie was the wench who brought out those last juleps. Did you notice her? I thought so. Millie's noticeable, as niggers go. But she ain't what she was in her young days. Millie's turned forty-eight. Did you ever see the beat of that sassy carriage? And those eyes! She hates me as she wouldn't the devil himself, and she takes delight in showing it. That proves how easy I am with them. Of course I could break her will, but up to about now I've had to keep her in good condition for business reasons. And she knows it, so there you are. But my time's coming.

I don't usually sell under fifteen—can't get the price. But some kind of fate was after Millie's children. Again and again I'd have offers for hers when they wa'n't over five or six—offers it would be a sin and against nature to refuse. Why I've had the price I'd expect to get for the full-grown nigger, offered me for her brats when they couldn't do a thing beyond picking up a handkerchief! I don't wonder, in a way. Millie's a creole nigger, and three-fourths white herself. Most of her brats have been lighter yet, and that pert and pretty they'd be singled out from the whole litter of pickaninnies by every man who came here. So whenever a pickaninny was wanted, it generally came from Millie's brood.

It went along and went along, and some fate kept singling out her brats and carrying them off at anywhere from five to eight years. She actually hasn't kept a child over eight years, except the lame one. First off, it was purely a matter that fate attended to. I sold them because no man in his right mind would have refused the offers I had for them. But latterly I've played fate some myself. She roused my dander after a time, you see. I think I would sell a brat of Millie's at a sacrifice if it got over eight, but I've not needed to, so far. She's the most profitable nigger I ever had even if she did cheat me out of four years' returns. That happened this way. Millie had her first brat at fifteen. Well along about thirty-five or so, she got the very devil in her and no mistake. She'd had eighteen children in those twenty years, and the iron had entered her soul, it seems. What d'you say? Well, she is an exception. But any way, she's three-fourths white. She ought to have some notion of "white" feelings. As I was saying the iron had entered her soul, for she only had the three youngest left. You'd have thought three'd have kept her contented, but there's no reason in these niggers. I swear before God that up to that time I had never sold a brat of Millie's to tantalize her, but she insisted I had and she wouldn't get out of the notion.

Well for three years if you please, that wench was barren. Time went on and on but no sign of any more of Millie's. The doctor couldn't make it out. I always keep a doctor on the place. When you breed niggers, it pays his salary a dozen times over to keep them looked after and right up in prime condition. Now you know it's unheard of for a nigger wench to go barren at thirty-five. But at last she lost her head and got to boasting that she'd bear no more children for me to sell down the river. So then I knew how to bring her round. The youngest of her brats was three, so I looked out for a chance and sold the three at one lick. This time I did do it a-purpose, and what's more I told her so. I thought afterwards that the easiest way to have brought her to terms would have been to have threatened to sell them, but I'm quick-tempered. I didn't stop to think it all out, just paid her back in her own coin. The impulse took me by the throat, so to speak, and right on top of that the opportunity came and I seized it. Then I had Millie on my hands for a while I can tell you. She was like a wild devil. I had to have her watched for days for fear she'd kill herself or me. When we finally came to terms I had to promise her, that if she ever had a child that was imperfect in any way she might keep it. I thought I was safe to promise that, but by God, sir, the next brat she had had a twisted foot. I don't know how it happened. The niggers claimed she used voodoo charms. At any rate there's the fact. So that made four years she didn't do her duty by me. Never, since I bought my first nigger forty-one years ago, have I been so riled toward one of them as I am toward her. I've held my hand for business reasons, but I needn't do that much longer. My turn's coming. I'll make a field nigger of her pretty soon and keep her there till she's ready to go down on her knees and beg my pardon for what she's done, and own up that she's lived like a queen all her life and never knew it. I'll see to it that she gets the airs and sassiness welted out of her. Oh, I'll break her yet! But meantime fate has had another fling at her. By God, sir, it's preposterous, the way that wench has caught it from all sides, after all. She's got exactly one child now. A brat about seven months old.

Yes, that's what I'm going to tell you, what happened to Jim. I kept my word and didn't sell him. He was worth more to keep Millie good-natured and up to her duty, any way. Besides, I never had an offer for her clubfooted cub. But mind you, about a year ago Jim came back from an errand to another plantation and brought the measles. Now this is where fate comes in again, flat-footed. Jim died, and the two Millie had left died. She only had two, fortunately, for I've kept hers sold down pretty close the last ten years. But not another pickaninny on the place, though most of them had it, took any harm from it.

Talk about fate! I tried to make Millie see that the Lord was punishing her for not having done her duty in that state of life in which it had pleased Him to place her. Millie got religion four or five years ago, and I thought that ought to be just the argument to touch her heart, but she only spit at me. I mean exactly that, spit at me. It makes them mighty sassy, these wenches, when they think they're so valuable for breeding purposes that you won't beat them. I've made it a rule to keep business considerations first, but Lord, I don't quite know how I've happened to stick it out in her case.

Oh, yes, Millie realizes that her breeding days are about over. But she thinks I'm going to sell her. I always sell 'em with their last brat you see, while they're still useful, and she knows that. There isn't an old negress on the place. And Millie thinks, d'you see, because I have put up with her impudence for business reasons, that I shall go right on and sell her, just the same as any other wench, at a certain age. But no; I sha'n't sell Millie. I've got a few scores against her, and I guess I can afford to settle them. No, she isn't a field hand yet. This last brat of hers needs her for a while still.

Well, as I was saying, that's the way fate looked after Jim and the two others. I lost two likely niggers that time. I don't count Jim among my losses, but it's always been a sort of consolation to me that Millie lost him too. She took on like mad at the time, and if she hadn't found religion good and strong, I don't know what methods we could have used to calm her down. But after a time, sir, she had the impudence to tell me that she was glad the Lord took them before I had a chance to sell them down the river. I've chalked that up against her, too. She spends her time between praying the Lord for deliverance and for vengeance on me. As if the Lord interfered in the affairs of niggers. I can't notice that he concerns himself particularly with the affairs of white folks. It's all chance—and business ability.

Yes, yes, perhaps the Lord did interfere when he sent you along to get my little shaver out of the danger his fool of a nurse had let him into. My God! If I lost him! He's the only one I ever had. I didn't marry till fifty-five, and I shouldn't have then if I hadn't wanted an heir.

Eh! Oh, they don't count. Do you suppose any southern gentleman takes account of *them*, when he makes his will?

Sell Millie? Zounds, man! Haven't I made it plain that she's had my dander riz these fifteen year, so's it's made it hard for me to keep a cool business head where she's been concerned? She's going to the cotton field just as soon as the cotton's ready to pull. That nigger's *got* to knuckle down to me on her bended knees, if I have to half kill her to get her there. I'll break her as I'd break a wild horse. Do you suppose I've bided my time, and stood her impudence for business reasons, to be done out of my turn at the last moment?

I know, I know, I understand my debt to you,

sir. If you hadn't got to the little chap just when you did—my God, I'd have let my whole bunch of niggers go, when I saw the slim chance he had. But ask me anything else. Anything in reason, sir, and it's yours.

Zounds! I knew you were a preacher, a preacher and a northerner. Why did I have to babble to you about the wench Millie? Our southern clergymen, sir, preach the Bible, sir—that a slave should be subject to his master in all things!

Well, you've got me down, sir, I won't deny it. But I won't sell Millie. If that's the only way I can square my big account with you, I'll give her to you, sir. Yes, and the brat. Lord! This comes near being more than I can stand! What'll you do with her?

Well, by the great horn spoon!

If anybody had told me last week, that I'd give Millie away to a preacher from New York who was going to set her free I'd have killed myself laughing at him! By God! I would, sir!

I've a notion the Lord has took notice of Millie's prayers at last. I'd never have believed it. Here's her "deliverance." But there ain't any vengeance on me in sight, I'm relieved to notice.

It's a remarkable coincidence, sir! If you hadn't had the nerve and grit to do what you did for the little lad, when it might have meant death for both of you sir—oh, I appreciate your courage, sir, b'Gad, I do! And if, on the top of that, I hadn't let my tongue wag like an old fool's about Millie—

Well, I'm sorry. I'll make no bones of that. But I pay my debts of honor on demand. On demand, sir. Millie's yours. Yes, and the brat.

I'll make out the papers in the morning.

Lo! Desire is potent.
But endless its waxing and waning
Till with Justice (called Love) it be blent,
the True Path attaining.

JARED WILLSON

Being
Incarnation the Tenth
of the Soul
Osru

Jared Willson, staunch union man, took advantage of the prolonged applause to slake his thirst from the contents of the white stone-china pitcher at his elbow. He drew the back of his hand across his mouth, brushed the hand absently against his right trouser leg, and faced his audience again.

His eyes blazed with strong personal feeling. Somehow his subject was a little out of hand to-night; had the bit in its teeth and was dragging him along. For one thing, the day was an anniversary of great sadness to him and memory had been torturing him cruelly.

" 'Taint fer no milk-and-water, mushy-wushy sentimental reasons, nor yet fer fear—you know me, all of you, and you know it aint fer fear,—that I'm telling you to leave vengeance out of the matter and go in fer justice, jest plain, unadulterated justice. You kin safely leave the vengeance to Gawd—He's looking out fer that—and don't you fergit it! But look out fer yerselves, that there aint no vengeance owin' t'you, fer you'll surely git it, here or hereafter, here or hereafter.

"So what I say is this. If it'll improve the conditions of you and yer mates in any way—really improve them—to smash a damned millionaire, why smash him. Blow him up with dynamite if you want; only be damn sure that getting him out of the way is a reel step toward justice." (Applause.)

"As sure as there's a Gawd in heaven, and there is, they'll all pay up for their sins, now or by and by. I've been a Christian fer fourteen years but I don't want none of this here 'only believe on the Lord and your sins shall be washed whiter than snow' religion. No, comrades, the Gawd I believe in is a just Gawd. Let the mercy go, I say. Or else, make it mercy fer the sinned against and justice fer the sinner." (Applause.)

"If you git very free with yer mercy to the sinner, the sinned against is tolerable likely not to git even justice done *him*. Justice is all I want, and justice is what I'm willing to take fer whatever I've done, and justice I'll work for, night and day, till I drop dead." (Applause.)

"So don't you waste no valyble time, like our esteemed friend the last speaker, growling about the good times the men who rob you of your earnings are having with their ill-gotten gains. They'll pay. As sure as there's a Gawd they'll pay, measure fer measure, an eye fer an eye, and a tooth fer a tooth. The old Jews was right about it. The Gospel is true too, but it don't really give the lie to the plain, sound justice of an eye fer an eye and a tooth fer a tooth, as some of these here mushy preachers says it does.

"You won't find nothing in the words spoken by our blessed Lord himself to interfere with every feller getting his just deserts. You just look again ef you think so.

"But I didn't set out to preach no sermon, lads. Excuse me all. What I wanted to say is this. Do you think that skinny old devil of a kerosene thief, fer instance, is going to pray himself out of any of the sufferin' that is his due fer the way he's made the victims of his rascally business methods suffer? Not one jot, not one tittle. Till all be fulfilled. Eternity is plenty long. He'll have time to suffer pang fer pang, fer every pang he's ever caused any one. And he can't plead, 'Oh, Lord! I didn't know I was doin' it!' neither, fer he knows well enough when he's doin' as he wouldn't like to be done by and that's plenty to fix the blame on him.

"I don't believe in no eternal hell, because there wouldn't be no justice in letting a man go on sufferin' after he'd felt as much pain as he'd caused, but I guess it'll take most of eternity to square the accounts of some men. His sort, f'instance. Why, take jest one case, that happened to come beneath my notice. This devil forced a man to shut down. This man wouldn't sell when he wanted him to—you know the trick—so when he had him hipped he refused to buy. Teach the other chaps a lesson, you know.

"There was one man who had worked for the man he had busted up, who couldn't get no other job. Too old, you know. This man had a wife and a granddaughter. They starved for a while, and then the girl got tired of that and drifted onto the street and broke their hearts. Years of shame and sufferin' fer three people—and only Gawd Almighty knows how many more suffered, one way or another, from that one foxy business trick—and a few more thousands a year more than he can spend fer the old cheat that planned it and put it through. Now ther' aint no just Gawd that'll let him off fer one second of the sufferin' he caused them three. If 'twas twenty years apiece, that makes sixty fer him. Measure fer measure, a tooth fer a tooth.

"No, there aint no Gawd that washes away yer sins till they're paid fer—don't you bank on it a minute. There may be heaven, there probably is, though I aint no good on figurin' out what it's like. But I'm sure about hell. It's needed fer his kind and bunches of others as bad in various ways. But I'm preachin' again. I aint myself tonight!"

(Cries of "Go on!")

"When I got religion I got conviction of sin, but I didn't want nothin' but justice even fer myself. I'm willin' to suffer for every bit of pain I ever caused. I don't want no fergiveness' fer my sins—justice is plenty good enough fer me. I tell you what, there's nothin' like knowin' you've got to square your own account some time or other to make you careful what you do. There's nothin' equal to it in the namby-pamby 'only believe and your sins shall be blotted out forever' religion. I tell you, no believing will blot out a single sin. They'll be blotted out as fast as you've paid fer them in kind; paid fer them in kind!" (Applause.)

Jared Willson wiped the sweat from his forehead with his palm, and shook the drops from his hand.

"Some of you young chaps have been talking up this strike in the wrong sperit. You'd think, to listen to some of you, that the only reason for a strike was to cripple the capitalists and give them less money to spend on their pleasures. Fool's logic! But after all, it's just your unsatisfied sense of justice that's putting you wrong. Your heads is queered but your hearts is right. Don't get the notion in your minds that it's your business to spoil the fun of the men who are spending your rightful money. You've got bigger business than that I hope. 'Vengeance is mine; I will repay, saith the Lord.' And He don't need no help of yours, neither. If a man deserves death He can drop a flower-pot on his head as he passes along the street. Or tip him over a cliff in the auto that he bought with your money. He don't need none o' your bombs, *He* don't. If a man deserves torment, and he's to get some of his Hell right here, the Lord kin let loose on him with some horrible disease that will burn like hell fire.

"I won't say no more about it. You kin work it out fer yerselves. But keep it clear in your heads that what you're workin' fer is justice fer yourselves and yer fellows, and leave justice fer yer oppressors to work itself out. There's a hereafter and they'll get their dues. Oh, they'll get what is coming to them, don't you fret. I should go clean mad, when I remember what I've suffered through no fault of mine, if I didn't have that blessed faith in a just Gawd to tie to. His strong right arm will overtake every one of the devils who have made my life a hell for nigh onto thirty years."

He choked up and fell silent a moment. He was thinking of his petted Janet, just turned sixteen who, nine years ago that night, had died the victim of some ruthless, unknown tramp.

" 'The Lord do so to me, and more also,' if I've ever done a hundredth part of the meanness and evil that's been done to me. I don't want nothin' better fer myself than that same justice I want to see visited on the heads of my enemies.

" 'With whatsoever measure ye mete'—remember that—'with whatsoever measure ye mete.' "

"Tell me a story, Jack!"

"You know them all, Sis."

"You fibber! Three years in Cuba and home a week—not a week yet—and you've told me all your stories already! Oh, Jack! Begin!"

She perched on the arm of his chair and forcibly conveyed his pipe from his languid fingers.

Jack laughed.

"All right, Kitten. I'd forgotten what a dictatorial infant you were. Give it here. I can't talk without it. Now stop whisking the flies off my chin with the end of your pigtail, that's an angel child. Better make me comfortable when you want a story, there's a straight tip for you. What sort of story?"

"About some man who was brave. About the bravest man you saw in the whole three years."

Jack smoked with irritating deliberation.

"Isn't there one who was braver than the rest?"

"There's one I think was braver than the rest. I don't know whether you'll see it, Kate."

"Go on, Jack. What did he do?"

"He hardly comes up to specifications; not the conventional ones,—the ones you judge heroes by. He didn't make any spectacular grand stand play, you know. I believe he had about six lines in the paper handed him afterwards. That's all I ever saw. He didn't look like a hero, either. He looked like the sort of man that works in gangs on buildings. A mason, perhaps; certainly no higher."

"Oh, Jack!"

"I'm not treating you very well, am I, Kate? Well, this is a story from life, and life isn't so very picturesque." He picked up her "Morte d' Arthur" that lay on the veranda railing. "If you don't like my hero go back to Mallory, with his dinky Sir Percivales and Sir Launcelotes. We can't compete with him now-a-days."

Kate laughed and pinched his cheek till he screwed up his face in protest. "If he's a hero I shan't mind his being a workman."

"How good of you! You wouldn't have approved of his manners. He was a rough old fellow who swore about as often as you say, 'How perfectly dreadful.' "

"How perfectly dreadful!"

"Exactly. And he swallowed some whiskey straight about as often as you drink water."

"Hm!" sniffed fastidious Kitty, who was just old enough to begin to have views on the liquor habit.

"You don't like the sort my hero is? Too bad. And what's more, he was by no means cleanly in his habits. I never saw him when he didn't have dirty finger nails—"

Katherine put a firm hand over his mouth.

"Now that's enough, Jack Ryder. If he's a hero, tell me about it and quit fooling."

"Fooling, young lady! I'm merely giving you a faithful pen picture! But all right. We'll skip the rest of the personal description if you want to. You're too young to appreciate it, that's the matter." He caught her chastising hand and held it.

"You know we had the deuce of a time cleaning Cuba up. And especially we had to wipe out the yellow fever before they would let us come home. You knew about that, or at least you thought you did. You know that after a while we found that the regular Egyptian plague of mosquitoes they have down there carried it."

"I read all about that," quoth Katherine, feeling very well informed.

"You haven't the least idea what fools the Cubans were. Every year when the season came round they used to lie down and die, as thick as flies and as meek as good old Moses. They never thought for a second there was anything to be done about it."

"Were you sorry you were a doctor then?" questioned Kitty.

"No," said Jack shortly, his face darkening. He remembered how he had had to set his teeth when he started for the quarantined pavilions, until habit came to his aid and he could go there without thinking what he was doing.

"Some of the experiments we had to try got into the papers. Not all of them, though. Some of them weren't very dangerous and some of them were. This one was."

"What one?"

"The one," said Ryder, "that we tried on the old mason who didn't clean his finger nails."

"Oh!" said Katherine. And then, "Did he die?"

Jack looked carefully enigmatic.

"I suppose you've picked up the habit of turning over to read the last page. Don't you know that spoils the story?

"West—he was still the Surgeon-General then—posted that he wanted a volunteer, and what for. Generally when he asked for volunteers he got 'em—right off the bat. But this time there were just about nine chances out of ten that the volunteer would have a soldier's funeral, d'you see, Kitten? How do you like my hero now?"

"Did he die?"

"Do you have to die to be a hero?" evasively. "Well there weren't any takers for two or three days, and that's a long time for one of Uncle Sam's calls for volunteers to go begging. Then this old chap came around to headquarters and asked for Dr. West. West was out and they handed him over to me. He hadn't come to volunteer exactly, he had a lot of questions to ask first. But it wasn't long before I saw he was really going to do it. I was sorry for the old boy, it looked to me so like a dead sure miss for him, and much as we needed his help I talked against it. Do you remember Mettus Curtius?"

"Of course. I adored him," said Kate, winking away the unwelcomed tears.

"Don't cry, Kitten. I'm just telling you a hero story, that's all.

"Every time he was off duty he'd hunt me up with more questions to ask. He knew exactly what he was doing, you know. There wasn't any hot-headed, impulsive, 'hurrah boys' physical courage about it. It was just cold-blooded walking up and shaking hands with death. That's a lot harder, Kate.

"I used to ask him why he was going to do it and what do you think he said? 'I don't know. I've never done nothin' fer nobody.' Doesn't sound much like Sir Percivale-Launcelot, eh, Kittie?"

"Stop about Sir Percivale-Launcelot!"

"All right. And then he would go on quizzing me about what would come of it if we found out what we wanted to find out, and what it would do in the long run towards cleaning up Cuba. He was a wise old bird. Always every five minutes or so, I'd remind him that it was quite on the cards that he wouldn't pull through and he would shrug his shoulders and go on asking the keenest questions, till he knew just about as much about it as I did."

"Was he very unhappy? Had he gone to war because he wanted to get killed?" asked Kate, remembering the heroes of some score of novels.

"No. He liked living well enough. He just kept saying that he never had done nothing for nobody. The courage bug had bitten him I guess, Kitten," pinching her cheek as he saw the tears start again. "Too bad about his double negatives, isn't it, Toots?"

"A truly hero can use any kind of grammar he likes," declared Kate stoutly.

"Right! They'll never make a snob of you, Sis!"

"Well?" prompted Katherine.

"He was a psychological problem," mused Jack aloud, forgetting her. "He wasn't the sort heroes are made of at all—not that kind. Brute courage, maybe. Sticking to his engine till it was ditched—that, yes. Not the Mettus Curtius type."

"Did he die?" asked Kittie, her eyes widening.

Jack took out a clipping and showed it to her. "The papers didn't get at all of it. If they had, he'd have had the whole of their first pages at least once."

> Jared Willson, one of the soldiers who volunteered to be inoculated by the bite of a mosquito that had previously bitten a yellow fever patient, is dead. He was one of six who answered the recent call of Surgeon-General West to submit to inoculation, and experimental curative treatment in case yellow fever developed. The incident has proved beyond question that Yellow Jack has been repeatedly transmitted by mosquitoes. It is thought certain that the other five will recover. Willson is a martyr to science.

"There, there, Kitten!" sopping her eyes with his handkerchief. "Don't you suppose they take good care of heroes when they get them over on the other side?"

AFTERWORD

And suddenly the Shining One was with me.

Far, dizzily far below us reeled the world. I put my hand out timidly and grasped a fluttering end of his garment. For I saw that I had no wings and I was very sore afraid. The earth swung past below us and we trod lightly upon—what?

He looked into my eyes, smiling serenely, and withdrew his raiment gently. And straightway I was ashamed that I had known fear.

He said: "Is not God—?"

Then I smiled also, and floated gladly beside him. (Shoulder to shoulder, the angel and I, even as two brothers.)

And he said: "You have seen what you desired to see."

"I have seen."

"And you have understood?"

I answered: "I could not have believed that out of so much evil good would come!"

Said the Shining One: "What is Evil?" And I was dumb before him.

Then he said: "What is Good?"

And still I was dumb.

He looked at me with searching eyes that

probed to the roots of my being. And suddenly a light stole in upon my soul and I made exultant answer.

"All is as God would have it!"

Said the Shining One: "Even so!"

We swept through space together, two sons of God, gloriously exulting, thrilling to the dominant chord of the universe.

All is even as God would have it!

I looked below me again. The earth was no longer there, so far had we fled through space. Neither were there stars, nor any other planet. And there was nor darkness nor light, yet I saw the Shining One.

And I said: "It is well with that man but—"

"But—?"

I plead for him.

"But he does not know it is well with him!"

The inscrutable, smiling eyes of the Shining

One answered somewhat, but I could not fathom their meaning.

"If he might but know what I know!" I pleaded. And again.

"Even if he must straightway forget it, and go back to the bitterness of earth blind, deaf, to all we twain understand!"

The tears rained from my eyes.

"I see well that he must not remember, else no pain could ever again hurt him! Yet will it strengthen him a little to know for a moment, and the strength will remain."

I cried aloud.

"He has great need of strength. The path he has chosen has little light and his feet will be bruised often."

I found courage to stoop and kiss the hand of the Shining One, humbly supplicating.

Then the Shining One answered me.

"Those lives you re-lived but now were yours."

I hid my eyes with my hands and fell through space, for an eternity. The seraph swept down beside me.

Afterwards, I uncovered my face and looked up. The smile of the Radiant One was even as before, inscrutable, all-comprehending, ineffably gentle. He said:

"It is given to all, on the eve of returning to embodiment, thus wholly to understand."

And I said to him then:

"All is well, for all is as God wills it! I will go back there now, to endure whatever it is just that I should endure. But I am fain, if this be possible, to suffer all it remains for me to suffer in one life and so bring it to an end."

The Radiant One grew of a sudden more dazzling, as though joy streamed from him, and he said:

"Even so you chose, the last time you drew near the earth seeking rebirth. Behold, that former desire and the fruits thereof are accomplished. It is now given you to desire anew."

Marvelling, I thought aloud: "I do not understand!"

He smiled.

"What would you fain do when you return to the flesh?"

I trembled.

"That which I choose—will come to pass?"

"Desire is potent."

I found no words.

"And also the fruits of desire are ever to be well thought upon."

Then I answered with passion:

"I would that I might harm no one! Though it slay me; though I must walk through fire for untold ages to avoid offense; yet I choose it rather; yea, a thousand times rather!"

Then for the last time the Resplendent One smiled down upon me.

"You have chosen well. But—does it suffice, to harm no one? Yet is it a step on the Path. Rest here in peace, for the moment of your return to earth is not fully come."

He is gone

I can hear the singing
of the worlds hurling themselves through space

it is granted me to perceive how their orbits
interlace everlastingly

THIS EXCLUSIVE EDITION

has been typeset for The Reincarnation Library
in Weiss Titling, Weiss Roman and Italic,
and printed by offset lithography
on archival quality paper at
Thomson-Shore, Inc.

The text and endpapers are acid-free and meet
or surpass all guidelines established by
the Council of Library Resources
and the American National
Standards Institute™.

Book design by Charlotte Staub